To: Faith

Enjoy your life
one bite at the time!

Obrigado!

Helena's
Portuguese
Kitchen

Editor: Emilie Mongrain
Graphic design: Josée Amyotte
Computer graphic design: Johanne Lemay
Photo adjustment: Johanne Lemay
Copy Editor: My-Trang Nguyen
Proofreading: Lynne Faubert
Photograph: Tango
Cooking Stylist: Jacques Faucher
Translation: Lynne Faubert with Josée Lafrenière

Bibliothèque et Archives nationales du Québec and
Library and Archives Canada cataloguing in publication

EXCLUSIVE DISTRIBUTORS:

For Canada and the United States:
MESSAGERIES ADP*
2315, De la Province St.
Longueuil, Québec J4G 1G4
Tel.: 450-640-1237
Fax: 450-674-6237
Internet : www.messageries-adp.com
* subsidiary of the Sogides Group Inc.,
   a subsidiary of Québecor Média Inc.

For France and other countries:
INTERFORUM editis
Immeuble Paryseine,
3 Allée de la Seine
94854 Ivry Cedex
Tel.: 01 49 59 11 56/91
Fax: 01 49 59 11 33
Orders:
Tél.: 02 38 32 71 00
Fax: 02 38 32 71 28

For Switzerland:
INTERFORUM editis SWITZERLAND
P.O. Box 69 - 1701 Fribourg - Switzerland
Tel.: (41-26) 460-80-60
Fax: (41-26) 460-80-68
Internet : www.havas.ch
E-mail : office@havas.ch
Distribution : OLF SA
Z.I. 3, Corminbœuf
P.O. Box 1061
CH-1701 Fribourg
Orders :
Tel.: (41-26) 467-53-33
Fax: (41-26) 467-54-66

For Belgium and Luxembourg:
INTERFORUM BENELUX S.A.
Fond Jean-Pâques, 6
B-1348 Louvain-La-Neuve
Téléphone : 32 (0) 10 42 03 20
Fax : 32 (0) 10 41 20 24
Internet : www.interforum.be
Courriel : info@interforum.be

10-15

Printed in Canada

Legal deposit: 2015
Bibliothèque et Archives nationales du Québec

ISBN 978-1-988002-15-6

Government of Québec - Tax credit for book publishing
– Administered by SODEC – www.sodec.gouv.qc.ca

The publisher gratefully acknowledges the support
of the Société de développement des entreprises
culturelles du Québec for its publishing program.

 Conseil des Arts **Canada Council**
du Canada **for the Arts**

We gratefully acknowledge the support of the Canada
Council for the Arts for its publishing program.

We acknowledge the financial support of the
Government of Canada through the National
Translation Program for Book Publishing, for our
translation activities.

We acknowledge the financial support of the
Government of Canada through the Canada Book Fund
for our publishing activities.

HELENA LOUREIRO

Helena's
Portuguese Kitchen

80 simple & sunny recipes

JUNIPER
PUBLISHING
A Quebecor Media Corporation

CONTENTS
Conteúdo

THE PLEASURES OF DISCOVERY 9

HORS D'OEUVRES & STARTERS 11

SOUPS & SALADS 37

FISH 65

SEAFOOD 91

MEAT & POULTRY 117

SIDES 147

DESSERTS 173

BASIC RECIPES 197

GOOD ADDRESSES 209

RECIPES INDEX 211

THE PLEASURES OF DISCOVERY
O prazer da descoberta

Some passions begin in childhood. My love of cooking has been with me for as long as I can remember. .

As soon as I could read and write, I started transcribing every recipe I found inspiring. I eventually accumulated an impressive number of them in stacks of notebooks.

Then I went from theory to practice. I was interested in improving recipes by using less of some ingredients or adding new ones, or by varying cooking times. In this way, through experimentation, I came to create a whole collection of authentic Portuguese dishes that say something about me and my culture.

The love for my heritage led me to become an accomplished chef and a proud ambassador of Portuguese cuisine. I hope this book will give you a taste of what my native land has to offer.

My heritage has also made me a devoted mother, and I want to share my passion with the two people dearest to me: my sons, Daniel and Diogo.

Meus meninos, isto é para vocês. Amo-vos mais que tudo!

Helena

HORS D'OEUVRES & STARTERS
Aperitivos e entradas

PETISCOS PLATTER

Prato de petiscos

SERVINGS: 4
PREPARATION: 15 MINUTES
MARINADE: 4+ HOURS
COOKING: 10 MINUTES

100 g (3.5 oz) pork cutlets
Oil (for the barbecue)
100 g (3.5 oz) *chouriço* (chorizo)
100 g (3.5 oz) Portuguese black
   pudding
2 whole red bell peppers
4 country-style dinner rolls
Portuguese cheese shavings (hard or
   semi-hard cow's milk cheese) (see
   note 2)
Parsley, chopped
Piri-piri mustard, to taste (see note 3)
Piri-piri sauce, to taste

MARINADE

2 tbsp lemon juice
1 to 2 garlic cloves, chopped, to taste
Piri-piri sauce, to taste
1 tbsp smoked paprika
125 ml (½ cup) white wine
60 ml (¼ cup) olive oil
2 bay leaves
2 tsp dried oregano
Sea salt
Fresh ground black pepper

NOTES

1. Petiscos *are Portuguese
appetizers usually served
as a nibble—with aperitifs or
at a cocktail party.* **2.** *São Jorge or
Castelões cheese, for example.*
3. *Portuguese mustard is spiced
with piri-piri sauce. You can find
it in Portuguese grocery stores or
make it yourself, see recipe p. 205.*

MARINADE PREPARATION

In a bowl, whisk together marinade ingredients. Transfer to a large resealable bag. Add pork cutlets, close bag and knead until meat is well coated. Let macerate in refrigerator at least 4 hours.

Preheat barbecue on high and oil grate.

Remove pork cutlets from marinade. Place cutlets, *chouriço*, black pudding and bell peppers on hot grate, and grill 3 to 5 minutes on each side until desired doneness.

Remove food from barbecue and cut into chunks. Serve right away in a large platter, sprinkled with cheese shavings, and dinner rolls on the side. Garnish with chopped fresh parsley. Accompany with piri-piri mustard and piri-piri sauce.

SARDINE BALLS

Almôndegas de sardinhas

SERVINGS: 12
PREPARATION: 25 MINUTES
REFRIGERATION: 30 MINUTES
COOKING: 20 MINUTES

SARDINE BALLS

1 kg (2 lbs) frozen sardines, thawed, well cleaned and gutted (see note)
100 g (⅔ cup) cooked rice
Juice of ½ lemon
1 garlic clove, chopped
¾ tbsp parsley, chopped
¾ tbsp cilantro, chopped
1 tsp Espelette pepper
Sea salt
Fresh ground black pepper

TOMATO SAUCE

2 tbsp extra-virgin olive oil
1 medium onion, chopped
1 red bell pepper, cut in strips
2 garlic cloves, chopped
500 g (1 lb) ripe tomatoes, blanched, peeled and seeded
125 ml (½ cup) water
2 tbsp parsley, chopped
2 tbsp cilantro, chopped
2 bay leaves

NOTE
Fresh or frozen sardines can be found at good fishmongers.

Sponge dry the sardines and finely chop flesh using a knife or food processor.

In a bowl, combine sardine meat, rice, lemon juice, 1 garlic clove and the parsley and cilantro. Season with salt, pepper and Espelette pepper, mixing well. Cover and cool in refrigerator for at least 30 minutes.

While mixture is chilling, prepare tomato sauce. In a pan, heat oil and sauté onions, bell pepper and chopped garlic. Add in tomatoes, then season with salt and pepper. Let simmer around 10 minutes over medium heat.

Form balls with sardine preparation. Place fishballs in hot tomato sauce and add up to 125 ml (½ cup) water to dilute a little. Cover and cook over low heat around 10 minutes, gently stirring until fishballs are cooked and hot. Serve immediately.

BRAISED SQUID

Ensopado de lulas

SERVINGS: 4
PREPARATION: 15 MINUTES
COOKING: 30 MINUTES

22 garlic cloves, minced
1 onion, thinly sliced
3 tbsp extra-virgin olive oil
1 tbsp smoked red-pepper paste (see note 1)
125 ml (½ cup) white wine
500 g (1 lb) ripe tomatoes, finely diced
500 g (1 lb) squid, cleaned
2 tbsp capers
2 tbsp fresh parsley, chopped
Fresh ground black pepper
Piri-piri sauce, to taste
Sea salt

NOTES
1. You will find smoked red-pepper paste in fine food stores. 2. Served on a good slice of bread, these simple tasty tapas will make you feel like you're enjoying cocktails by the seaside.

In a pot over very low heat, cook garlic and onion in olive oil for around 3 minutes or until onion is translucent. Season with salt, pepper and smoked red-pepper paste. Pour in wine and reduce by half. Add in tomatoes, squid, capers and parsley. Simmer uncovered over very low heat for 25 minutes.

Season with a few drops of piri-piri sauce, if desired, and serve on a slice of toasted bread.

OCTOPUS CARPACCIO WITH CITRUS

Carpaccio de polvo

SERVINGS: 4
PREPARATION: 20 MINUTES

500 g (1 lb) cooked octopus, thinly
   sliced (see p. 51)

LAMB'S LETTUCE & CITRUS SALAD
100 g (5 cups) lamb's lettuce
200 g (1 cup) citrus supremes
   (clementine, orange, lime, lemon)
Parsley, chopped, to taste
Chives, chopped, to taste
Cilantro, chopped, to taste
2 tbsp your choice of citrus juice
60 ml (¼ cup) extra-virgin olive oil
2 tbsp raspberry vinegar

CHICKPEA & SQUID-INK MASH
1 can (540 ml/19 oz) chickpeas, drained
   and rinsed (or see p. 206 for how to
   cook dried chickpeas)
Juice of ½ lemon
125 ml (½ cup) extra-virgin olive oil
2 garlic cloves, minced
1 tbsp squid ink (see note)
Espelette pepper, to taste
1 tbsp fresh parsley, chopped
Fleur de sel
Fresh ground black pepper

NOTE
Squid ink is the black liquid ejected by some cephalopods that serves to colour ingredients when cooking. You will find it at some fishmongers.

PREPARING CHICKPEA MASH
In a food processor, combine chickpeas, lemon juice, olive oil, garlic, squid ink, a little fleur de sel and black pepper. Process around 2 minutes or until mash is smooth and homogeneous. Sprinkle with Espelette pepper and chopped fresh parsley.

Spread chickpea mash in a large platter. Top with slices of cooked octopus.

PREPARING LAMB'S LETTUCE SALAD
In a large salad bowl, place salad ingredients and toss until leaves are well coated in oil and vinegar.

Garnish octopus carpaccio with lamb's lettuce and citrus salad, then serve.

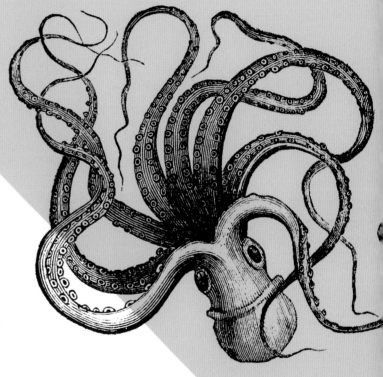

OCTOPUS

Polvo

This little creature with a noteworthy texture is a queen of the Mediterranean. It is often avoided because people believe it's too difficult to work with—but that's not the case. Served fresh in a carpaccio or grilled to perfection with the slightest hint of salt, this exquisite sea dancer provides a delicate flavour deserving of our attention. As the young Napoléon Simard-Proulx once told me, «Octopus is the filet mignon of the sea.» I couldn't agree more!

LOBSTER ROLLS WITH FRESH VEGETABLES

Corneto de lagosta e legumes

SERVINGS: 6
PREPARATION: 15 MINUTES

Zest and juice from 1 lemon
200 g (1 cup) extra-fine green beans, sliced lengthwise in 2 (or 4 if bigger)
2 medium carrots, julienned
3 potatoes, cooked and julienned
75 g (½ cup) green peas, cooked
2 eggs, hard-boiled
2 tbsp pitted black olives
3 tbsp chives, minced
3 tbsp fresh parsley, chopped
1 kg (2 lbs) lobster meat, cooked
125 ml (½ cup) mayonnaise
6 kale leaves, blanched

In a bowl, gently mix lemon zest and juice, vegetables, eggs, olives, fresh herbs and lobster meat. Add in mayonnaise and stir carefully until ingredients are well coated.

Divide salad between blanched kale leaves and roll to form small cones. Serve.

BLACK-COD GRAVLAX

Gravlax de bacalhau preto

SERVINGS: 4
PREPARATION: 15 MINUTES
MARINADE: 24 HOURS

1 tbsp black peppercorns
1 tbsp coriander seeds
3 tbsp sugar
3 tbsp coarse salt
1 kg (2 lbs) skin-on black-cod fillets
Zest of 1 lime
60 ml (¼ cup) liquor or vodka

Pour peppercorns and coriander seeds in a mortar and crush coarsely using the pestle. Transfer spices to a bowl, then mix with sugar and salt.

Line the bottom of a large rectangular dish with plastic wrap. Place cod on top, skin side up. Spread spice mixture evenly over fish, pressing down so that spices penetrate slightly. Sprinkle with liquor (or vodka), top with zest, then wrap fish tightly in plastic wrap.

Place a small cutting board or plate on top of fish, then add a can to weigh it down. Chill in refrigerator for 24 hours.

Remove plastic wrap and discard brine juices. Gently pat dry fish using paper towels to remove most of the spice mixture. Quickly rinse fish under running cold water, if needed.

When ready to serve, slice cod flesh diagonally into paper-thin slices without cutting the skin. Remove skin and discard.

If desired, serve as is or as a garnish for minty cream of green pea soup (see recipe p. 153), with *chouriço* chips on the side (see recipe p. 199).

PRESUNTO & CHEESE-STUFFED BREAD LOAF

Pão recheado com presunto e queijo

SERVINGS: 4
PREPARATION: 15 MINUTES
COOKING: 20 MINUTES

1 country-style loaf of bread
1 garlic clove, chopped
3 tbsp parsley, minced
2 tbsp extra-virgin olive oil
150 g (1 cup) raclette cheese, grated (or any other cheese that melts well when warmed)
50 g (¼ cup) presunto (Portuguese ham), cut in small cubes (see note)
50 g (¼ cup) cooked ham, cut in small cubes
1 *chouriço* (chorizo), cut in small cubes
4 tbsp homemade mayonnaise (see recipe p. 205)

NOTE
You may replace presunto *with any other dried, smoked cold cut.*

Preheat oven to 190°C (375°F).

Slice top off bread loaf and scoop out centre completely.

In a small bowl, mix together garlic, parsley and olive oil with a small spoon. Add grated cheese, *presunto*, ham and *chouriço*. Add mayonnaise and mix until ingredients are well blended.

Stuff bread loaf with this mixture and cover with aluminum foil. Bake in oven for 20 minutes.

Serve with bread croutons and a crisp vegetable salad.

LEEK & CHOURIÇO TARTS

Pasteis de nata salgados

YIELD: 12 TARTS
PREPARATION: 30 MINUTES
RESTING: 24 HOURS (SEE NOTE)
COOKING: 15 MINUTES

35 g (¼ cup) flour (for work surface)
300 g (10 oz) puff pastry, homemade or
   store-bought (see note)
2 tbsp extra-virgin olive oil
100 g (⅔ cup) *chouriço* (chorizo), diced
200 g (2 ¼ cups) leeks, white part only,
   finely diced
3 egg yolks

250 ml (1 cup) heavy (35%) cream
1 tbsp parsley, chopped
Piri-piri sauce, to taste
Sea salt
Fresh ground black pepper

NOTE
*It is better to prepare and mould
dough the day before.*

Flour work surface. With a rolling pin, roll out puff pastry as finely as possible, then roll back on itself to form a large cylinder. Cut into rounds, 2.5-cm (1-in) wide.

In muffin moulds, place a round of dough in each cavity. With slightly wet fingers, press on dough so it lines the bottom and goes up the sides evenly. Let stand at room temperature for 24 hours, so dough won't puff up during cooking and remain very flaky.

Preheat oven to 180°C (350°F).

In a pan, heat olive oil over medium heat and cook *chouriço* a few minutes until slightly golden. Add in leeks and cook, stirring non-stop with a wooden spoon. Add a few drops of water to help with cooking and let simmer for 2 to 3 minutes more. Remove from heat and let cool.

Pour lukewarm mixture into a food processor and mix until creamy. Transfer to a bowl. Add in egg yolks, cream and parsley. Season with salt, pepper and piri-piri sauce to taste. Mix using a spatula.

Divide mixture between muffin moulds. Bake around 10 minutes or until crust turns golden.

Remove from oven and let cool. Serve as a side for soup or as an appetizer.

PEPPERS STUFFED WITH GOAT CHEESE

Pimentos recheados com queijo de cabra

SERVINGS: 4
PREPARATION: 15 MINUTES
COOKING: 30 MINUTES

4 red bell peppers, well rinsed
150 g (1 cup) fresh goat cheese
3 tbsp parsley, chopped
4 slices *presunto* (dried Portuguese ham),
   thinly sliced (see note)

ARUGULA SALAD WITH PINE NUTS
25 g (1 cup) arugula
3 tbsp pine nuts
2 tbsp extra-virgin olive oil
Red wine vinegar, to taste
Fleur de sel

NOTE
You may replace presunto with any other dried, smoked cold cut.

Preheat oven to 180°C (350°F). Place peppers directly on middle oven rack. Roast for around 30 minutes, or until skin peels off and peppers are very soft.

Meanwhile, combine goat cheese and parsley in a small bowl. Reserve.

Remove peppers from oven and let cool until they are easier to handle. Cut them in 2, then remove seeds and white membrane carefully so as not to tear flesh. Stuff each half with cheese-parsley mixture, then wrap in a slice of *presunto*.

PREPARING ARUGULA SALAD
Combine arugula and pine nuts in a salad bowl. Reserve.

In a small bowl, whisk together olive oil with a few drops of vinegar and fleur de sel. Pour dressing over salad and mix gently.

Serve peppers with salad on the side.

TUNA, SARDINE & CRAB RILLETTES

Rillette de atum, caranguejo e sardinhas

SERVINGS: 12 AS APPETIZERS
PREPARATION: 10 MINUTES

2 cans (125 g/4 oz each) whole light tuna in olive oil
2 cans (125 g/4 oz each) sardines in spicy tomato sauce
100 g (¾ cup) crabmeat
200 g (¾ cup) cream cheese
1 green onion, minced
½ bunch cilantro, minced
1 tsp ginger, grated
3 tbsp lemon juice
Piri-piri sauce, to taste
Sea salt

In a salad bowl, crush tuna with a fork, then mix with sardines and crabmeat. Add in cheese, then green onion, cilantro, ginger and lemon juice. Crush with the fork until all ingredients are well-blended. Season with salt and piri-piri sauce to taste. Serve on croutons or crackers.

REINVENTED SEAFOOD TERRINE

Terrina de mariscos reinventada

SERVINGS: 6
PREPARATION: 25 MINUTES
COOKING: 45 MINUTES

100 g (1 ½ cup) bread, crusts removed,
    torn into small pieces
750 ml (3 cups) water
4 tbsp extra-virgin olive oil
2 garlic cloves, chopped
2 tbsp cilantro, chopped
400 g (14 oz) medium-size shrimp,
    cut in small pieces
200 g (7 oz) mussels,
    cut in small pieces

200 g (7 oz) clams, cut in small pieces
100 g (1 cup) crabmeat,
    cut in small pieces
4 egg yolks
Butter (for the ramekins)
Apple white butter (for serving)
    (see recipe p. 199)
Fleur de sel, to taste
Fresh ground black pepper

In a large bowl, soak bread in water for a few minutes. Squeeze bread with your hands to remove excess water. Reserve bread in a plate and discard water.

In a large skillet, heat olive oil, then sauté garlic, 1 tbsp chopped cilantro and seafood around 10 minutes or until well cooked.

Add bread and cook for another 5 minutes. Bind with the egg yolks. Season with salt and pepper to taste.

Preheat oven to 190°C (375°F). Butter six ramekins.

Divide preparation among ramekins and sprinkle with remaining cilantro. Place ramekins in a large roasting pan, then pour water into pan until water reaches halfway up the sides of the ramekins. Bake in oven around 30 minutes or until terrines are lightly golden.

Unmould and arrange each terrine in a dinner plate. Sprinkle with a little apple white butter and serve with a salad on the side.

SOUPS
& SALADS
Sopas e saladas

ALENTEJO-STYLE GASPACHO

Gaspacho alentejano

SERVINGS: 4
PREPARATION: 30 MINUTES
CHILLING: 1 HOUR

12 clams, well cleaned
3 tbsp extra-virgin olive oil
125 ml (½ cup) white wine
600 g (1 ⅓ lbs) very ripe tomatoes
2 red bell pepper, seeded and finely diced
1 cucumber, peeled and diced
1 onion, chopped
1 garlic clove, chopped
60 ml (¼ cup) extra-virgin olive oil

25 g (⅓ cup) bread (without crust), torn into small pieces
80 ml (⅓ cup) red wine vinegar
Few drops piri-piri sauce (optional)
Fresh oregano, chopped
Cilantro, chopped
Sea salt
Fresh ground black pepper

NOTE
Oregano and cilantro, the fresh herbs used in this recipe, are typical of the Alentejo region and give this gaspacho a fresh new twist.

COOKING CLAMS
Place clams in a large pot with 3 tbsp olive oil. Add white wine, cover and cook over high heat until clams open. Remove from heat. Discard unopened clams and reserve others.

PREPARING VEGETABLES
Make an X-shaped cut at the base of tomatoes. Place them in a large pot of boiling water for 1 minute or so, until their skin bursts. Transfer immediately to a large bowl of icy water and let cool for a few seconds. Remove tomato skins with a small knife. Cut flesh into pieces and seed.

Combine tomatoes, peppers, cucumber, onion and garlic in a large salad bowl. Add olive oil and mix. Season with salt and pepper, then chill 1 hour in refrigerator.

PREPARING GASPACHO
In a blender, combine crustless bread, red wine vinegar and all the vegetables with their juices. Blend a few minutes until smooth. (Gaspacho must be very creamy.)

Pour mixture in a soup tureen. Season with salt, pepper and a few drops of piri-piri sauce, to taste.

Garnish soup with clams. Sprinkle with chopped oregano and cilantro. Drizzle with a little olive oil and serve.

SUMMER VEGETABLE SOUP WITH ROMANO BEANS

Sopa de feijão Romano

SERVINGS: 4
PREPARATION: 20 MINUTES
COOKING: 40 MINUTES

1 L (4 cups) vegetable broth
400 g (1 cup) fresh shelled romano beans
2 tbsp extra-virgin olive oil
1 onion, diced
2 garlic cloves, minced
3 carrots, peeled and diced
1 leek, diced
3 tomatoes, peeled and diced
4 Savoy cabbage leaves, sliced in 1-cm (½-in) strips
1 tbsp flat-leaf parsley, chopped
Olive oil (for serving)
Sea salt
Fresh ground black pepper

In a pot, bring broth to a boil over high heat. Add beans. Cook for 15 to 20 minutes or until beans are al dente (i.e. still a little firm when bitten into). Remove from heat and reserve.

In a large pot, heat half the olive oil over medium heat. Add onion and garlic, then sauté for 10 minutes. Add carrots and leek, then cook for 2 minutes. Add tomatoes, beans and the vegetable broth used to cook them.

Bring to a boil. Add cabbage and parsley. Cover, reduce heat to low and simmer 10 minutes or until carrots are tender.

Season with salt and pepper to taste. Divide soup among bowls. Drizzle with a little olive oil and serve

STONE SOUP

Sopa da Pedra

THE STORY

A finalist among the seven wonders of Portuguese cuisine, Sopa da Pedra is a typical soup of Portugal, and in particular the town of Almeirim. Located in the heart of the Ribatejo region, Almeirim is considered the "capital of stone soup."

Traditionally, one places a very clean stone in a deep dish or large bowl used to serve the soup. Once the meal is over, it's customary to keep the stone for the next time the soup is made.

SERVINGS: 4 TO 6
SOAKING: 24 HOURS
PREPARATION: 30 MINUTES
COOKING: AROUND 1 HOUR

1 bay leaf
Piri-piri sauce
250 g (1 ¾ cups) dried red kidney beans, previously soaked (see note 1)
2 pieces pork knuckles, around 100 g (3.5 oz) each
50 g (1.5 oz) lardons
1 small black *chouriço* (chorizo)
1 small *chouriço* (chorizo)
2 garlic cloves, chopped

1 onion, chopped
5 tbsp olive oil
2 potatoes, peeled and diced
1 carrot, diced
1 turnip, diced
½ bunch kale, cut in chunks
1 small bunch cilantro, chopped
1 tbsp white vinegar
Sea salt
Fresh ground black pepper

NOTES

1. *Pre-soak beans for 24 hours in a bowl of cold water to rehydrate them. Use 2 parts of water for 1 part of beans.* **2.** *A unique dish, Sopa da Pedra is a very rich and aromatic soup, perfect for welcoming guests to your home or when the weather turns frigid.*

PREPARATION

Pour 2 L (8 cups) of water in a large pot. Season with salt and pepper. Add bay leaf and a few drops of piri-piri sauce. Add kidney beans, pork, lardons and *chouriços*. Bring to a boil, reduce heat and let simmer around 45 minutes.

With a slottled spoon, remove bay leaf, pork, lardons and *chouriços*. Cut pork into pieces and *chouriços* into rounds. Reserve.

In a large pot, sauté garlic and onion in olive oil for a few minutes. Add diced potato, carrot and turnip. Incorporate beans and their cooking juices. Cook for 20 minutes over medium heat.

Remove pot from heat and blend soup lightly using an immersion blender. Add chopped meat, *chouriço* rounds and kale. Sprinkle with chopped cilantro, add vinegar and mix. Serve very hot.

TOMATO VELOUTÉ

Sopa de tomates

SERVINGS: 4
PREPARATION: 10 MINUTES
COOKING: 25 MINUTES

1 garlic clove, minced
1 onion, minced
3 tsp extra-virgin olive oil
500 g (1 lb) very ripe tomatoes
200 g (2 cups) cherry tomatoes, cut in 2
2 potatoes, peeled and cut in chunks
1.5 L (6 cups) chicken broth
1 tbsp tomato paste
Fresh parsley, chopped, to taste
2 tbsp crème fraîche
Sea salt
Fresh ground black pepper

NOTE
This delicious soup can also be enjoyed cold. To prepare it, I use very ripe tomatoes, plus cherry tomatoes for sweetness. I add potatoes to make an unctuous velouté.

In a large pot, sauté garlic and onion in olive oil. Add tomatoes, cherry tomatoes and potatoes. Pour in chicken broth and season with salt and pepper.

Bring to a boil, reduce heat, mix in tomato paste and cook for 15 minutes or so, until potatoes are tender.

Transfer to a blender and purée until nicely smooth.

Divide velouté among bowls and sprinkle with chopped parsley. Garnish with a touch of crème fraîche and serve with a good slice of toasted bread.

ASPARAGUS SALAD WITH ROASTED ALMONDS, SÃO JORGE CHEESE & SERRANO

Salada de espargos, São Jorge e Serrano

SERVINGS: 4
PREPARATION: 15 MINUTES
COOKING: 10 MINUTES

ALMOND CREAM
120 g (1 cup) almond powder
125 ml (½ cup) milk

DRESSING
125 ml (½ cup) extra-virgin olive oil
2 tbsp raspberry vinegar
¼ lemon
1 tbsp piri-piri mustard (see note 1)
1 tbsp honey
1 garlic clove, chopped
Sea salt
Fresh ground black pepper

SALAD
28 asparagus
1 to 2 tbsp extra-virgin olive oil
35 g (¼ cup) roasted almonds
   (see note 2)
30 g (¼ cup) São Jorge cheese shavings
   (see note 3)
Few slices serrano ham (Iberian
   prosciutto)

NOTES
1. *Portuguese mustard is spiced with piri-piri sauce. You will find it in Portuguese food stores or you can make it yourself, see recipe p. 205.* **2.** *To roast almonds, arrange on a cooking sheet and put in the oven at 180°C (350°F) for about 10 minutes, until they dry and brown slightly.* **3.** *São Jorge is a cow's milk cheese. Made in the island of São Jorge in the Azores, it's a typical authentic cheese of Portugal's terroir.*

PREPARING ALMOND CREAM
Combine almond powder and milk in a blender, then mix on high for 10 minutes or so. Scrape down the sides with a spatula regularly. Reserve.

PREPARING DRESSING
In a small bowl, emulsify oil and vinegar. Add remaining ingredients, whisk and rectify seasoning.

PREPARING SALAD
With a paring knife, peel the stalks from 20 asparagus. Slice them lengthwise using a mandolin. Place slices in a large salad bowl. Reserve.

In a skillet, roast remaining 8 asparagus for 3 to 4 minutes in a little olive oil. Reserve.

Pour dressing over raw asparagus and mix well. Add roasted almonds.

In a serving platter, spread almond cream and arrange roasted asparagus on top. Garnish with raw asparagus and almond salad. Sprinkle with São Jorge cheese shavings and a few slices of serrano ham. Serve.

LOBSTER, CAULIFLOWER SEMOLINA, CILANTRO & CLEMENTINE SALAD

Salada de lagosta

SERVINGS: 4
PREPARATION: 45 MINUTES
COOKING: NONE

2 lobsters, cooked
½ cauliflower
½ red bell pepper, finely diced
2 tbsp cilantro, chopped
2 tbsp fresh mint, chopped
3 green onions, minced
Lemon zest, to taste
2 tbsp tobiko (see note)
Sea salt
Fresh ground black pepper

CLEMENTINE SALAD DRESSING
125 ml (½ cup) extra-virgin olive oil
3 tbsp clementine juice
Lemon zest, to taste
Piri-piri sauce, to taste
Sea salt

NOTE
Tobiko is the Japanese name for flying fish roe. You will find it at your fishmonger.

Shell lobsters. Keep claws for decoration. Dice meat and reserve in refrigerator.

Break cauliflower into pieces and place in a food processor. Pulse to a fine semolina texture (similar to couscous).

In a large bowl, combine cauliflower semolina, pepper, cilantro, mint, green onions and lemon zest. Season with salt and pepper. Add diced lobster and *tobiko*. Reserve.

PREPARING CLEMENTINE DRESSING
Mix dressing ingredients in a small bowl. Pour over salad and mix. Decorate with lobster claws and serve.

OCTOPUS & BROAD BEAN SALAD

Salada de polvo

SERVINGS: 4 TO 6 (SEE NOTE)
PREPARATION: 30 MINUTES
COOKING: 1 HOUR 40 MINUTES

1.5 kg (3 lbs) octopus (preferably whole)
2 red onions, peeled
500 g (1 lb) whole tomatoes
1 bay leaf
1 to 2 tbsp extra-virgin olive oil
50 g (½ cup) *chouriço* (chorizo),
    cut into rounds
1 red onion, minced
100 g (1 cup) baby potatoes, cooked
135 g (1 cup) fresh or frozen broad
    beans, cooked
1 red bell pepper, cut into strips
150 g (1 cup) cherry tomatoes,
    each cut in 2

Juice of ½ lemon
Sea salt
Fresh ground black pepper

DRESSING
80 ml (¾ cup) olive oil
2 tbsp red wine vinegar
Sea salt
Fresh ground black pepper

FOR SERVING
12 confit garlic cloves (see note p. 171)
4 tbsp flat-leaf parsley, chopped

NOTE
*You can also serve this salad
as a starter. In that case,
plan 1 large tentacle for 6 portions.*

COOKING OCTOPUS

Thoroughly clean octopus under running water and detach tentacles from head. In a large pot of salted water, place the 2 onions, tomatoes and bay leaf. Bring to a boil, add octopus, reduce heat to low and simmer 1 hour and 15 minutes. Remove octopus from broth and let cool.

In a skillet, heat olive oil and brown *chouriço* rounds. Add 1 minced red onion, potatoes, broad beans and cherry tomatoes. Let simmer over low heat for 5 to 10 minutes. Add a splash of lemon juice and continue cooking until the skin of tomatoes splits. Reserve.

Preheat barbecue on high and oil grate.

Cut cold octopus into large chunks. Season with salt and pepper, then coat with olive oil.

Place octopus on hot grill and cook over high heat for 3 minutes on each side to create grill marks. (You can also broil octopus in the oven.)

Meanwhile, in a bowl, combine dressing ingredients.

In 4 plates, divide vegetables and grilled octopus pieces. Pour over dressing and sprinkle with parsley. Add 3 confit garlic cloves per plate.

GREEN PEA & RADISH SALAD

Salada de ervilhas e rabanetes

SERVINGS: 4
PREPARATION: 10 MINUTES
COOKING: 5 MINUTES

200 g (1 ¼ cups) fresh green peas
90 g (¾ cup) carrots, thinly sliced with a mandolin
50 g (½ cup) radishes, thinly sliced
Juice of ½ lemon
Olive oil, to taste
Sea salt
Fresh ground black pepper

In a pot of boiling water, cook green peas for 5 to 6 minutes, then chill in a bowl of icy water. Drain.

In a large salad bowl, combine all the ingredients. Serve immediately.

ROASTED-POTATO SALAD

Salada de batatas grelhadas

SERVINGS: 4
PREPARATION: 20 MINUTES
COOKING: 10 MINUTES

SALAD
2 roasted red bell peppers
1 kg (2 lbs) fingerling potatoes,
   cooked in their skin
8 confit cherry tomatoes
   (see recipe p. 168)
10 whole pearl onions
75 g (½ cup) pitted black olives

ROASTED-LEEK MAYONNAISE
Oil (for cooking sheet)
2 leeks
2 egg yolks
1 tbsp Dijon mustard
2 tbsp lemon juice
1 tbsp honey
2 tbsp red wine vinegar
2 tbsp extra-virgin olive oil
Parsley, chopped, to taste
Sea salt
Fresh ground black pepper

NOTE
You can also roast the pepper on the barbecue, over high heat, until skin chars slightly. Transfer to a bowl, cover and let cool before peeling. Rinse under running cold water, pat dry and cut into strips.

ROASTING PEPPER
Preheat oven to 200°C (400°F).

Place pepper directly on middle oven rack and bake 20 minutes or until skin starts to wrinkle. Remove from oven, transfer to a bowl, cover and let cool before peeling. Rinse under cold running water, pat dry and slice into strips.

PREPARING MAYONNAISE
Preheat oven to 200°C (400°F).

Lightly oil cooking sheet. Arrange leeks on cooking sheet and season with salt and pepper. Place in oven and roast for around 10 minutes. Remove cooking sheet from oven and cut leeks into large chunks.

In a blender, combine egg yolks, mustard, lemon juice, honey, vinegar and roasted leeks. Purée until smooth. Gradually blend in olive oil until the consistency of mayonnaise. Incorporate chopped parsley. Season with salt and pepper to taste.

PREPARING POTATO SALAD
Combine salad ingredients in a large serving bowl. Add mayonnaise, mix well and serve.

PICKLED SARDINE & GREEN APPLE SALAD

Salada de sardinhas com maças

SERVINGS: 4
PREPARATION: 20 MINUTES
MACERATION: 35 MINUTES
COOKING: 1 MINUTE

375 ml (1 ½ cups) water
2 tbsp sea salt
20 fresh sardine fillets
3 tbsp raspberry vinegar
2 green apples, thinly sliced
20 g (1 cup) arugula
3 shallots, peeled and minced
2 fresh tomatoes, diced
4 tbsp extra-virgin olive oil
2 tsp parsley, minced
Fresh ground black pepper, to taste

In a shallow dish, combine water and sea salt. Place sardines in this brine and macerate for 15 to 20 minutes.

Drain sardines, rinse under cold water and gently pat dry with paper towels.

In the shallow dish, marinate sardines for 15 minutes in raspberry vinegar. Dry, cut in 2 and reserve.

Meanwhile, boil a pot of water and blanch green apples for 1 minute. Drain and pat dry.

Line the bottom of a large salad bowl with arugula, then place apples, pickled sardines, shallots and tomatoes on top. Drizzle with olive oil, sprinkle with parsley and season with pepper.

SARDINES

Sardinhas

They may be small in size but they're long on taste, and they're festive too! Sardines in oil, grilled sardines or salad sardines—we can't do without these salty delicacies. Take advantage of their popularity in Portuguese cuisine to put them back on your menu or to discover this gem you may have overlooked for too long.

CAESAR-STYLE SALAD WITH *CHOURIÇO* & SARDINE DRESSING

Salada César e chouriço, vinagreta de sardinhas

SERVINGS: 4
PREPARATION: 15 MINUTES
COOKING: 15 MINUTES

20 Brussels sprouts, leaves removed
6 slices cornbread (see recipe p. 158)
2 tbsp butter
1 egg yolk
1 tbsp lemon juice
1 garlic clove, minced
190 ml (¾ cup) extra-virgin olive oil
2 tbsp capers, chopped
1 can (125 g/4 oz) sardines, chopped
80 g (¾ cup) hard cheese, grated
    (São Jorge or Emmental, for example)
1 small romaine lettuce, hand-torn
16 *chouriço* chips (see recipe p. 199)
Fresh ground black pepper

Prepare a bowl of icy water.

In a pot of boiling salted water, blanch Brussels sprout leaves for 1 minute. Drain leaves and transfer to icy water to stop the cooking. Drain again and set aside.

In a large skillet, fry bread slices in butter on both sides around 1 minute. Set aside in a plate.

In a bowl, whip together egg yolk, lemon juice and garlic. Add around 60 ml (¼ cup) olive oil in a slow, steady drizzle, whipping non-stop. When mayonnaise starts to thicken, add remaining oil in a stream.
Add in capers and sardines. Incorporate one quarter of the grated cheese to this dressing and mix.

In a large salad bowl, gently mix Brussels sprout leaves, romaine lettuce and dressing. Add toasted cornbread and crispy *chouriço* chips. Toss gently. Sprinkle with remaining cheese, season with salt and serve right away.

WARM ENDIVE SALAD

Salada morna de endivias

SERVINGS: 4
PREPARATION: 10 MINUTES
COOKING: 20 MINUTES

6 endives, leaves separated and cut in 2
4 cornbread slices, torn into pieces
3 tbsp spicy maple walnuts (recipe follows) (see note)
2 yellow apples
200 g (7 oz) smoked duck, sliced

BROWN BUTTER SALAD DRESSING
2 tbsp salted water
2 tbsp maple syrup
Juice of 1 lemon

SPICY MAPLE WALNUTS
120 g (1 cup) unsalted walnuts
3 tbsp granulated maple sugar
1 tsp fleur de sel
½ tsp cinnamon
4 tbsp dark rum
2 tsp vanilla extract
125 ml (½ cup) maple syrup
2 tbsp unsalted butter

NOTE
To save time, you could use store-bought maple-flavoured nuts instead.

PREPARING BROWN BUTTER DRESSING
In a saucepan, melt butter over low heat and let it brown (careful, it must not turn black). Add in maple syrup and lemon juice, mixing well. Remove from heat and keep warm.

PREPARING SPICY MAPLE WALNUTS
Preheat oven to 180°C (350°F). Line a cookie sheet with wax paper.

Spread walnuts in a single layer on prepared cookie sheet. Toast in oven around 10 minutes, stirring from time to time. (Keep an eye so nuts don't burn.) Remove from oven and reserve.

In a bowl, mix together maple sugar, fleur de sel and cinnamon. Reserve.

In a deep pot over medium heat, bring to a boil rum, vanilla extract, maple syrup and butter, then simmer around 5 minutes or until liquid reduces by half.

Mix in walnuts, then continue cooking and stirring around 3 minutes or until the bottom of the pan is almost dry. Remove from heat and immediately add in sugar, salt and cinnamon mixture. Mix until nuts are well-coated.

Spread spiced-up nuts on cookie sheet lined with a new sheet of wax paper and let cool.

PREPARING SALAD
In a large salad bowl, combine endives, torn bread and spicy maple walnuts. Peel apples, cut them into quarters and add them to the salad. Add smoked duck. Drizzle with brown butter dressing.

FISH
Peixes

COD & SWEET POTATO CAKES

Pasteis de bacalhau com batata doce

YIELD: 24 CAKES
PREPARATION: 20 MINUTES
COOKING: 1 HOUR

300 g (10 oz) whole sweet potatoes, well washed
300 g (10 oz) fresh cod
250 ml (1 cup) milk
100 g (1 ½ cups) crustless bread, torn into small pieces
2 garlic cloves, chopped

1 onion, minced
35 g (½ cup) parsley, chopped
2 eggs, beaten
Vegetable oil (for frying)
55 g (½ cup) bread crumbs
Sea salt
Fresh ground black pepper

In a large pot of lightly salted boiling water, cook sweet potatoes around 35 minutes or until tender. Drain. Peel potatoes and mash in a bowl using a fork.

In a small pan over medium heat, cook cod in milk for 5 minutes. Remove cod and keep milk warm. Remove bones and skin from cod (if needed), and flake flesh with a fork. Set aside.

Place torn bread in a large bowl, then pour warm milk over bread. Add garlic, onion, parsley and cod. With a fork, mix the whole into a batter. Add mashed sweet potatoes and mix again. Incorporate beaten eggs, then season with salt and pepper to taste.

In a deep fryer or pan, heat vegetable oil to 190°C (375°F). Spread bread crumbs in a plate.

Shape cod mixture in patties approx. 2.5-cm (1-in) round, then roll in bread crumbs. Fry a few cakes at a time in hot oil for 4 minutes or so until golden.

Drain cod cakes on paper towels and serve hot, with a nice green salad on the side.

COD, POTATO & BROCCOLI CASSEROLE

Bacalhau no forno com batatas e brócolos

SERVINGS: 4
SOAKING: 24 TO 48 HOURS
PREPARATION: 20 MINUTES
COOKING: 1 HOUR

1 kg (2 lbs) salted cod, previously desalted (see note)
3 garlic cloves, chopped
2 large onions, chopped
Olive oil
1.5 kg (3 lbs) potatoes, peeled and cut into rounds

125 ml (½ cup) milk
500 ml (2 cups) heavy (35%) cream
1 bunch parsley, chopped
1 broccoli, in flowerets
A few unpitted black olives
1 red bell pepper (see technique p. 55)

NOTE
Desalt cod 1 to 2 days before starting casserole. To do so, soak fish 24 to 48 hours in a bowl of cold water placed in refrigerator. Change water 3 to 4 times.

PREPARING CASSEROLE

Preheat oven to 180°C (350°F).

Bring a pot of water to a boil. Reduce heat to medium, add cod pieces and cook 10 minutes. Remove cod from water, transfer to a plate and let cool.

In a skillet, cook garlic and onion in a little olive oil. Remove from heat and reserve.

In a large pot of boiling water, cook potatoes until tender but not fully cooked. Drain and reserve.

Remove fish bones, then shred flesh with a fork. Reserve.

In a small pot, heat milk and cream over low heat.

Meanwhile, oil a baking dish and, in successive layers, stack half the cod, half the onion, half the chopped parsley, half the potato rounds and half the broccoli flowerets. Repeat with remaining half of ingredients, then pour in the warm milk-cream mixture. Bake in oven for 30 minutes or until fish is cooked and vegetables are very soft.

Remove from oven, sprinkle with a few black olives, roasted pepper strips and minced parsley. Serve.

COD WITH GREEN PEAS & POACHED EGGS

Bacalhau com ervilhas e ovos escalfados

SERVINGS: 4
PREPARATION: 20 MINUTES
COOKING: 30 MINUTES

1 medium onion, minced
2 garlic cloves, chopped
6 tbsp extra-virgin olive oil
3 ripe tomatoes, finely diced
750 g (1 ⅔ lbs) desalted cod (see technique p. 68)
750 ml (3 cups) chicken or vegetable broth
1 kg (2 lbs) frozen green peas
1 tsp piri-piri sauce
4 eggs
1 bunch cilantro, chopped
Sea salt

In a pan over medium heat, sauté onion and garlic in olive oil around
5 minutes or until golden. Add tomatoes, piri-piri and salt, then simmer
over low heat for 10 minutes. Add cod and chicken (or vegetable) broth.
Cover and simmer for 15 minutes.

Add green peas, cover and continue cooking around 8 minutes.

Break eggs one by one and carefully place on green peas so egg yolks stay
intact. Cover and let eggs poach around 3 minutes.

Serve hot, sprinkled with chopped cilantro.

COD

Bacalhau

We call it *fiel amigo*, meaning "faithful friend."
Cod is served at every meal and on most
occasions. In Portugal, we say we have 365 ways
to prepare this versatile fish—one for every day
of the year. We love cod in everything, from
omelettes in the morning to croquettes in the
evening. But any true Portuguese will tell you
that we like it best unadorned: simply grilled
and drizzled with a little olive oil.

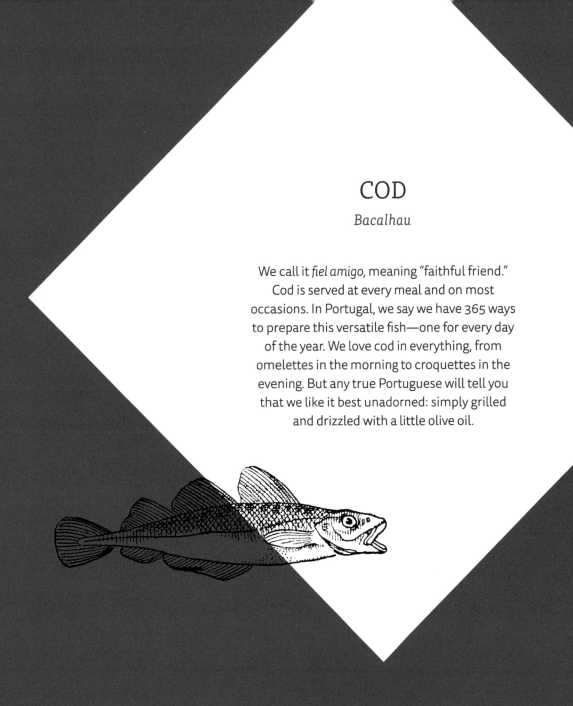

SABLEFISH CURRY

Bacalhau preto de caril

SERVINGS: 4
PREPARATION: 20 MINUTES
MACERATION: 1 HOUR
COOKING: 30 MINUTES

4 sablefish steaks, 125 g (4 oz) each (or your choice of any other white fish), rinsed and patted dry
1 bird's-eye chili pepper, minced
Juice of 1 lemon
1 onion, chopped
4 garlic cloves, chopped
2 tbsp fresh ginger, peeled and minced
4 tbsp extra-virgin olive oil
2 carrots, peeled and cubed

2 parsley roots (or 2 Jerusalem artichokes), peeled and cubed
1 red bell pepper, seeded and cubed
2 tbsp best quality possible curry powder
1 L (4 cups) chicken broth (or vegetable broth)
1 can (540 ml/19 oz) chickpeas, rinsed and drained
2 tbsp fresh mint, chopped
Sea salt
Fresh ground black pepper

Place fish steaks in a large airtight container. Season with sea salt, bird's-eye chili and half the lemon juice. Place in refrigerator around 1 hour.

In a pan, cook onion, garlic and ginger in 2 tbsp olive oil until tender. Add vegetables and curry powder, then continue cooking for 1 minute. Pour in broth and add chickpeas. Bring to a boil, reduce heat, cover and let simmer gently around 20 minutes or until carrots and parsley roots are tender. Season with salt and pepper.

In a non-stick skillet over medium heat, cook fish in 2 tbsp olive oil around 4 minutes on each side. Season with salt and pepper.

Divide vegetable mixture among four shallow dishes. Top with a fish steak, drizzle with remaining lemon juice and sprinkle with fresh mint. Serve immediately.

CORNBREAD-CRUSTED COD

Bacalhau com broa

SERVINGS: 4
PREPARATION: 15 MINUTES
COOKING: 35 MINUTES

2 medium onions, cut in rings
4 cod fillets, 125 g (4 oz) each
5 tbsp extra-virgin olive oil
Half cornbread (see recipe p. 158)
2 garlic cloves, chopped
2 tbsp black olives, chopped
5 tbsp parsley, chopped
180 g (1 cup) confit cherry tomatoes (see recipe p. 168)
1 tsp ground cloves
60 ml (¼ cup) white wine
Sea salt
Fresh ground black pepper

Preheat oven to 180°C (350°F).

Arrange onion rings in the bottom of an ovenproof dish. Place cod on top of onions, skin side up, then drizzle with olive oil. Bake in oven around 25 minutes or until cod turns a golden colour.

Meanwhile, in a bowl, crumble cornbread. Add garlic, olives, parsley, confit tomatoes and cloves. Season with salt and pepper, then mix. Pour in white wine and knead to a smooth, homogeneous batter.

Spread this batter over cod until the whole fish is covered by it. Return to oven and cook around 10 minutes or until crust is golden brown. Serve immediately.

FISH AND CHIPS-STYLE COD

Pataniscas de bacalhau

SERVINGS: 4
PREPARATION: 20 MINUTES
SOAKING: 1 HOUR
COOKING: 15 MINUTES

Vegetable oil (for frying)
500 g (16 oz) desalted cod (see note p. 68)
250 ml (1 cup) milk

TARTAR SAUCE
125 ml (½ cup) homemade mayonnaise
    (see receipe p. 205)
2 tbsp parsley, chopped
2 tbsp red onion, chopped
2 tbsp cucumber, finely diced
1 tbsp capers, drained and chopped
1 tbsp Dijon mustard
1 tsp piri-piri sauce
Sea salt
Fresh ground black pepper

BATTER
4 tbsp flour
1 tsp baking powder
170 ml (⅔ cup) pale ale
2 eggs
4 tbsp parsley, chopped
Sea salt
Fresh ground black pepper

Fill two-thirds of a frying pan with vegetable oil (or use a deep-fryer). Heat to 180°C (350°F).

In a large bowl, soak cod in milk for 1 hour.

PREPARING TARTAR SAUCE
In a bowl, mix all the ingredients. Chill.

PREPARING BATTER
In a bowl, combine flour, baking powder, beer, eggs and chopped parsley. Dip cod in batter to coat all over. Remove using a slotted spoon and transfer to a plate. Season with salt and pepper to taste.

With a spoon, place cod fillets in hot oil and fry for about 10 minutes, until brown and crispy.

Serve with tartar sauce and lemon wedges.

COD OMELETTE

Omelete de bacalhau

SERVINGS: 4
PREPARATION: 20 MINUTES
COOKING: 15 MINUTES

60 ml (¼ cup) extra-virgin olive oil
2 red bell peppers, julienned
2 potatoes, thinly sliced into rounds
300 g (10 oz) desalted cod or any other white fish
   (see note p. 68), shredded
2 garlic cloves, chopped
1 tomato, diced
1 sprig fresh parsley
20 g (1 cup) arugula
6 eggs
Sea salt
Fresh ground black pepper

In a skillet, heat 2 tbsp olive oil. Sauté peppers and potatoes for a few minutes. Add shredded cod, garlic, tomato, parsley and arugula, then continue cooking for 2 minutes.

Beat eggs in a large bowl. Season with salt and pepper. Add cod mixture to bowl and blend well.

Heat 2 tbsp olive oil in a large non-stick skillet. Once hot, pour in egg mixture and lightly rotate skillet to spread mixture evenly all over. Cook for 3 minutes without stirring, then turn omelette and cook the other side for 3 to 4 minutes, never stirring.

Cut into triangles and serve right away.

SWORDFISH *PICA-PAU*

Espadarte à Pica-Pau

SERVINGS: 4
PREPARATION: 15 MINUTES
MACERATION: 1 HOUR
COOKING: 20 MINUTES

400 g (13 oz) swordfish, cut in small cubes
4 garlic cloves, chopped
1 tbsp paprika
6 tbsp extra-virgin olive oil
190 ml (3/4 cup) moscatel (sweet Portuguese wine)
5 tbsp fresh parsley, chopped
125 g (1 cup) pickled vegetables, to taste
    (optional; see recipe p. 204)
4 hard-boiled eggs
Sea salt
Fresh ground black pepper

Place fish cubes in a large airtight container. Season with salt, pepper, garlic and paprika. Chill in refrigerator for 1 hour.

In a skillet, heat olive oil over medium heat. Add fish cubes and fry around 2 minutes per side. Add moscatel and swirl skillet in mid-air until fish is well coated. Let sauce reduce by half. Remove from heat. Add parsley and garnish with pickled vegetables.

Divide the preparation between plates and top each serving with a hard-boiled egg. Serve with oven-baked potatoes on the side (see recipe p. 161).

EUROPEAN SEA BASS STEW

Ensopado de robalo

SERVINGS: 4
PREPARATION: 20 MINUTES
COOKING: 30 MINUTES

1 tbsp extra-virgin oil
2 onions, chopped
140 g (2 cups) mushrooms, sliced
1 green bell pepper, seeded and
   chopped
6 garlic cloves, fine chopped
1 can (540 ml/19 oz) whole tomatoes,
   chopped
250 ml (1 cup) chicken or vegetable
   broth

2 potatoes, peeled and diced
1 tbsp fresh thyme, chopped
1 tsp salt
½ tsp piri-piri sauce
¼ tsp ground pepper
4 European sea bass fillets, approx.
   125 g (4 oz) each (or other fish,
   see note)
2 tbsp fresh parsley, chopped
1 tbsp grated lemon zest

NOTE
*At the fishmonger,
ask for European sea bass,
striped bass or any other fish with
firm, moist flesh. European
bass comes from saltwater fishing
and not fish farms.*

In a large heavy-bottomed pan, heat oil over medium heat. Add onions and cook 5 minutes, stirring from time to time, until tender. Add mushrooms, pepper and 4 garlic cloves. Cook for 10 minutes, stirring once in a while, until vegetables are tender.

Add tomatoes, broth, potatoes, thyme, salt, piri-piri sauce and pepper. Bring to a boil, reduce heat, cover and let simmer for 10 minutes or until potatoes are al dente (in other words, with a little bite still).

Add fish fillets, cover and cook for 3 to 5 minutes, or until flesh flakes with a fork.

Meanwhile, in a bowl, combine parsley, lemon zest and remaining garlic.

Ladle fish stew in four warmed bowls. Sprinkle each serving with the parsley mixture and serve right away.

MONKFISH & CLAM RICE

Arroz de tamboril e amêijoas

SERVINGS: 4
SOAKING: 2 HOURS
PREPARATION: 20 MINUTES
COOKING: 30 MINUTES

200 g (7 oz) clams (approx. 20 small clams)
4 tbsp extra-virgin olive oil
600 g (1 ¾ lbs) monkfish fillets, cleaned and cut in pieces
1 medium onion, minced
1 red bell pepper, seeded and finely diced
2 tomatoes, diced
1 tbsp piri-piri sauce
2 bay leaves
300 g (1 ½ cups) long-grain rice
4 tbsp cilantro, chopped
Sea salt
Fresh ground black pepper

Place clams in a bowl of salted water and let them soak for 2 hours in refrigerator to remove sand. Drain claims, rinse well and drain again. Transfer them to a large pan and cover with water. Cook over medium heat around 6 minutes or until clams open. Drain clams without shelling and set aside cooking water.

In a heavy-bottom pan, warm 2 tbsp olive oil over high heat. Add monkfish pieces and fry for 3 minutes on each side. Remove from heat and season lightly with salt and pepper. Set aside in a plate.

In the same pan over medium heat, add 2 tbsp olive oil and sauté onion and pepper around 5 minutes. Add tomatoes, piri-piri sauce and bay leaves. Season with salt and pepper to taste.

Pour clam cooking water in a measuring cup. If needed, add enough water to make 750 ml (3 cups) of liquid altogether. Pour this liquid on vegetables in the pan and bring to a boil. Once liquid is boiling, reduce heat to low and add rice. Cook for 10 minutes. Add fish pieces and cook for 5 minutes more. Add unshelled clams, remove from heat and mix.

Sprinkle with chopped cilantro and serve.

GRILLED RED SNAPPER WITH PARSLEY SAUCE

Pargo grelhado com molho verde

SERVINGS: 4
PREPARATION: 15 MINUTES
COOKING: 10 MINUTES

1 whole red snapper, around 1 kg (2 lbs),
　　cleaned and trimmed
2 garlic cloves, minced
Juice of ½ lemon
Extra-virgin olive oil
Sea salt
Fresh ground black pepper

PARSLEY SAUCE
125 ml (½ cup) extra-virgin olive oil
2 tbsp red wine vinegar
4 tbsp red onion, minced
45 g (½ cup) parsley, chopped
2 tbsp capers
1 garlic clove, chopped

Preheat barbecue grill on high.

Whisk together parsley sauce ingredients in a bowl. Reserve.

Season fish with salt, pepper, garlic and lemon juice, then brush with olive oil. Place fish on hot grate and grill for 5 minutes on each side.

Transfer fish to a large serving platter and drizzle with parsley sauce. Serve with sweet potato *migas* (see recipe p. 157).

SEAFOOD
Frutos du mar

SQUID BOUILLABAISSE

Caldeirada de lulas

SERVINGS: 4
PREPARATION: 15 MINUTES
COOKING: 30 MINUTES

3 large onions, cut in 2 then sliced thin
5 ripe tomatoes, diced
1.5 kg (3 lbs) potatoes, peeled and sliced thick
1 green bell pepper, cut in strips
1 red bell pepper, cut in strips
3 garlic cloves, chopped
1 kg (2 lbs) squid, cut in rounds
125 ml (½ cup) extra-virgin olive oil
250 ml (1 cup) water
250 ml (1 cup) white wine
1 bunch parsley, chopped
2 bay leaves
3 tbsp tomato paste
1 tsp piri-piri sauce
Sea salt

In a pot, arrange alternating layers of onions, tomatoes, potatoes, green and red bell peppers, garlic and squid. Repeat until all ingredients have been used.

Drizzle with olive oil, water and wine. Add parsley, bay leaves and tomato paste. Season with piri-piri sauce and salt to taste.

Bring to a boil and let simmer around 30 minutes or until potatoes are tender. Adjust seasoning and serve very hot.

SHRIMP, CHOURIÇO & ROASTED-PINEAPPLE KEBABS

Espetada de camarão com chouriço e ananás

SERVINGS: 6
PREPARATION: 15 MINUTES
MARINADE: 2 HOURS
COOKING: 10 MINUTES

48 raw shrimp, size 13/15
2 mild *chouriços* (chorizos), each cut in 36 pieces
1 small pineapple, cut in 36 pieces
Bambou kebab sticks

MARINADE
190 ml (¾ cup) extra-virgin olive oil
Juice of 1 lime
1 tsp mild paprika
½ tsp ground ginger
3 tbsp whisky

NOTE
These kebabs can also be cooked in the oven at 200°C (400°F). Arrange them on a lightly oiled cooking sheet and cook in oven around 14 minutes, turning halfway. Shrimp should be pink and quite juicy.

In a large bowl, whisk together marinade ingredients. Set aside.

Peel shrimp, leaving the tail on. Add to marinade and move gently around to coat well. Cover bowl and place in refrigerator to marinate shrimp for at least 2 hours.

Meanwhile, soak kebab sticks in a bowl of water.

Alternating, thread ingredients on kebab sticks as follows: shrimp, pieces of *chouriço* and pieces of pineapple. Set aside.

Preheat barbecue grill on medium-high and oil grate.

Place kebabs on hot grill and cook for 3 to 4 minutes per side.

Serve two kebabs per guest.

SEAFOOD-STUFFED CABBAGE ROLLS

Trouxas de marisco

SERVINGS: 4
PREPARATION: 30 MINUTES
COOKING: 1 HOUR 15 MINUTES

12 large Savoy cabbage leaves
500 g (1 lb) your choice of seafood
    (shrimp, lobster, mussels, shelled
    clams and/or cleaned squid)
1 onion, chopped
3 slices bacon, chopped
2 tbsp extra-virgin olive oil
3 garlic cloves, chopped

750 ml (3 cups) tomato sauce
500 ml (2 cups) chicken
    or vegetable broth
150 g (¾ cup) long-grain rice
4 tbsp fresh parsley, chopped
12 whole slices bacon, cooked
A little coarse sea salt
1 tsp salt

With a knife, thin down the central stem running along the base of each cabbage leaf. Prepare a bowl of icy water.

In a large pot of boiling salted water, blanch cabbage leaves for 5 minutes or until tender. Drain leaves and transfer to icy water. Drain again and set aside.

Fill a pot with enough cold water to cover prepared seafood and bring to a boil. Season with coarse sea salt. Add the prepared seafood and cook around 10 minutes. Drain. If using mussels and clams, remove the shells. Cut all seafood into small pieces.

In a large skillet, sauté onion and chopped bacon in olive oil. Add garlic, half the tomato sauce, half the broth and rice, then let simmer around 10 minutes. Add seafood and mix well. Remove from heat and let cool enough to manipulate.

Preheat oven to 180°C (350°F).

Pour remaining tomato sauce and broth in the bottom of an ovenproof dish.

Take a little of the seafood preparation and shape like a cigar using your hands. Place this cigar in the middle of a cabbage leaf, fold in the sides and roll. Repeat until all the stuffing and all the cabbage leaves have been used.

Arrange cabbage rolls side by side in the baking dish. Top each roll with a slice of cooked bacon. Cover with aluminum foil and bake in oven around 45 minutes or until cabbage is melt-in-your-mouth tender.

SHRIMP WITH PORT

Camarões ao Porto

SERVINGS: 4
PREPARATION: 15 MINUTES
COOKING: 20 MINUTES

8 frozen tiger shrimp
375 ml (1 ½ cups) heavy (35%) whipping cream
375 ml (1 ½ cups) port wine
3 tsp piri-piri mustard (see recipe p. 205)
60 g (¼ cup) butter
Sea salt
Fresh ground black pepper

NOTE
Rather than discard shrimp shells, use them to flavour a soup or improve a sauce. You can even add them to rice cooking water. To do so, in a skillet over medium heat, cook shells in a little salted water for 20 minutes. Once cooked, purée in blender with their cooking liquid, then strain the mixture in a colander to collect all the liquid. You can freeze this flavoured water in small ice-cube trays to keep them handy at all times.

Peel shrimp while not fully thawed so that their shells are easier to remove (see note). Make an incision lengthwise along the back of each shrimp and remove the black vein with the tip of the knife. Season shrimp with salt and pepper. Set aside.

In a bowl, mix together whipping cream, port and mustard. Set aside.

In a skillet, melt butter over medium-high heat and fry shrimp for 3 minutes on each side, keeping an eye out to avoid burning the butter (it would give shrimp a bad taste). Reduce heat to low, pour in creamy port mixture and let simmer around 10 minutes. Rectify seasoning as needed.

Serve on a bed of white rice or *chouriço* rice.

GRILLED SEAFOOD
WITH HERB-GARLIC SAUCE

Mariscos grelhados com manteiga de alho

SERVINGS: 4
PREPARATION: 15 MINUTES
COOKING: 10 MINUTES

Oil (for grill)
1.5 kg (3 lbs) your choice of seafood (baby squid, giant
   prawns, sea scallops, octopus)

HERB-GARLIC SAUCE
5 tbsp salted butter
4 garlic cloves, minced
125 ml (½ cup) white wine
1 bay leaf
Juice of 1 lemon
4 tbsp parsley, chopped
Piri-piri sauce, to taste
Sea salt

NOTE
*You can also grill seafood in a
skillet on the stove, with a little
olive oil or a knob of butter.*

Preheat barbecue on high and oil grate.

PREPARING SAUCE
On the stove, in a non-stick skillet, melt butter over medium heat.
Add garlic, white wine and bay leaf, then cook for 3 minutes. Incorporate
lemon juice and parsley. Season with salt and piri-piri sauce to taste.
Keep warm.

Arrange all seafood on very hot barbecue grill and cook for 4 to 8 minutes
or so, depending on chosen seafood.

Serve grilled seafood immediately, with herb-garlic sauce on the side.

SEL DE MER

Sal do mar

Salt has been used in cooking for ages.
When preparing a Portuguese recipe,
sea salt should always be used because the sea
plays an essential role in our people's life.
Whether sea salt is used before grilling fish or
for putting the finishing touch on a lovely salad,
choose it both to give your recipe a unique flavour,
and as a salute to the big blue—that icon of the
Portuguese community.

PAELLA WITH SQUID INK RICE

Paelha com tinta de chocos

SERVINGS: 4
PREPARATION: 15 MINUTES
COOKING: 25 MINUTES

500 ml (2 cups) chicken broth
2 tbsp saffron
1 onion, chopped
1 garlic clove, minced
1 red bell pepper, finely diced
1 tbsp extra-virgin olive oil
150 g (¾ cup) black squid ink rice (see note 1)
300 g (10 oz) fresh large prawns (around 40), peeled
50 g (¾ cup) frozen green peas
3 tbsp cilantro, chopped
Piri-piri sauce, to taste
Sea salt
Fresh ground black pepper

NOTES

1. *Black squid ink rice can be found in fine food stores.* **2.** *To taste, you can add sliced chorizo, squid, clams, lobster or fish fillets to your paella at the same time as the prawns or slightly before if some of your selected ingredients take a little longer to cook.* **3.** *For a greater harmony of flavours, it is best to use a paella pan, sold in most kitchen supply stores. Otherwise, use a large 50-cm (20-in) skillet or pan at least 12-cm (5-in) high.*

Preheat oven to 180°C (350°F).

In a bowl, mix chicken broth with saffron. Reserve.

In a paella pan, sauté onion, garlic and pepper in olive oil. Deglaze with half the saffron-flavoured broth, bring to a boil and cook on high for 5 minutes. Reduce heat to low, add in rice and let simmer for 10 minutes.

Incorporate remaining saffron broth. Add in prawns, green peas and chopped cilantro. Season with salt, pepper and a little piri-piri sauce to taste, then stir. Finish cooking in oven around 10 minutes or until broth is fully absorbed.

Serve with lemon and saffron aioli (see recipe p. 198).

CLAMS & CHOURIÇO

Ameijoas com chouriço e milho

SERVINGS: 4
PREPARATION: 20 MINUTES
SOAKING: 1 HOUR
COOKING: 30 MINUTES

2 kg (4 lbs) clams
6 tbsp extra-virgin olive oil
5 garlic cloves, chopped
2 onions, chopped
1 large red bell pepper, diced
2 tomatoes, finely diced
250 g (8 oz) *chouriço* (chorizo), cut in thick rounds
1 tsp piri-piri sauce
125 ml (½ cup) white wine
A few lemon wedges
6 tbsp fresh parsley and/or cilantro
2 roasted corn cobs (or 350 g/2 cups frozen corn kernels)
Salt

Clean clams very well. To do so, place them in a large bowl, cover with water, add 1 tbsp salt and let soak for 1 hour in refrigerator so they expel their sand. Drain, rinse and drain again. Set aside.

In a large pan over medium heat, warm olive oil and sauté garlic for 2 minutes. Reduce heat to low, add chopped onion and pepper, then sauté until onion turns translucent. Add tomatoes and *chouriço*. Season with salt and piri-piri sauce, then add white wine. Continue cooking until *chouriço* is cooked, around 10 minutes.

Add clams, cover pan and cook, shaking pan several times, around 2 minutes or until clams open.

Pour preparation in a serving dish. Garnish with lemon wedges, chopped parsley and/or cilantro, and roasted corn.

Serve right away with nice chunks of fresh bread to dip into the broth.

BULHÃO DE PATO PASTA

Massa à bulhão pato

SERVINGS: 4
SOAKING: 2 HOURS
PREPARATION: 15 MINUTES
COOKING: 20 MINUTES

2 kg (4 lbs) fresh clams (see note)
125 ml (½ cup) + 2 tsp extra-virgin olive oil
400 g (10 oz) fresh short pasta
6 large garlic cloves, chopped
250 ml (1 cup) white wine
2 tbsp piri-piri mustard (see recipe p. 205)
Juice of ½ lemon
6 tbsp cilantro, chopped
Sea salt
Fresh ground black pepper

NOTE
*Clams can contain sand. Soaking
them for a long period of time
helps to clean them.*

In a large bowl of salted water, soak clams for 1 hour in refrigerator. Drain, rinse and drain again.

In a pot, pour 125 ml (½ cup) olive oil, add clams and cover. Steam over low heat around 2 minutes, or until clams open. Once clams are open, remove shells and set aside.

In a large pot of boiling salted water, cook pasta until al dente, according to package instructions. Drain and keep warm.

In the same pot over medium heat, sauté garlic in 2 tsp olive oil, stirring to avoid garlic turning brown. Incorporate white wine and piri-piri mustard, then let reduce by half. Add in lemon juice, cilantro and shelled clams.

Place pasta in a large serving platter and cover with clam sauce. Sprinkle with cilantro and black pepper.

FISH & SHRIMP PASTA

Massinha de peixe e camarao

SERVINGS: 4
PREPARATION: 20 MINUTES
COOKING: 20 MINUTES

1 L (4 cups) water
200 g (6.5 oz) monkfish medallion
200 g (6.5 oz) sea bass (or other white fish)
4 tbsp extra-virgin olive oil
1 medium onion, chopped
2 garlic cloves, chopped
½ green pepper, finely diced
½ red bell pepper, finely diced
4 ripe tomatoes, cut into pieces

125 ml (½ cup) dry white wine
1 tbsp tomato paste
Piri-piri sauce, to taste
300 g (2 ½ cups) short pasta (like macaroni)
12 medium-size shrimp, peeled
1 tbsp salted butter
Fresh mint, minced, to taste
Fresh ground salt

In a pot, boil 1 L (4 cups) water. Arrange monkfish and sea bass in a large deep dish. Pour boiling water over fish and reserve.

In a large pot, heat olive oil. Sauté onion with garlic and peppers. Incorporate tomatoes, wine and tomato paste. Bring to a boil and let simmer uncovered for 3 minutes. Season with salt and piri-piri sauce.

Reduce heat, add fish and their water, pasta and shrimp, then cook over low heat around 8 minutes or until pasta is al dente. If needed, add more water so that pasta remains quite moist.

Mix in butter. Sprinkle with fresh mint and serve very hot.

SEAFOOD STEW

Feijoada de mariscos

SERVINGS: 4
PREPARATION: 25 MINUTES
COOKING: 30 MINUTES

4 tbsp extra-virgin olive oil
2 onions, chopped
3 garlic cloves, chopped
1 red bell pepper, cut in strips
250 ml (1 cup) clam juice
250 ml (1 cup) dry white wine
4 large ripe tomatoes, cut in pieces
100 g (3.5 oz) squid, cut in rounds
16 clams (voir la note 108)
400 g (2 ½ cups) frozen lima beans (or white beans)

200 g (6.5 oz) large prawns, fresh or frozen, peeled
200 g (6.5 oz) sea scallops, fresh or frozen
24 mussels
1 tsp ground cumin
½ tsp ground cloves
2 bay leaves
½ bunch cilantro, chopped
½ bunch parsley, chopped
Piri-piri oil (see recipe p. 201)

In a large pot, heat olive oil. Sauté onions, garlic and bell pepper over medium heat around 5 minutes or until vegetables are tender. Pour in clam juice and wine, then bring to a boil. Let simmer for 5 minutes over medium heat, then incorporate tomatoes. Cook for 4 to 5 minutes over low heat, until tomatoes are hot.

Add squid and clams, then continue cooking around 10 minutes or until clams open. Add in lima beans, prawns, scallops, mussels, cumin, clove, bay leaf, cilantro, parsley and piri-piri oil, to taste. Cook another 10 minutes or so.

Adjust seasoning if needed. Serve very hot with rice on the side.

CREAMY LOBSTER & SHRIMP RICE

Arroz de lagosta e camarão

SERVINGS: 4
PREPARATION: 25 MINUTES
COOKING: 30 MINUTES

1 L (4 cups) fish stock
2 tbsp extra-virgin olive oil
2 tbsp salted butter
2 green onions, minced
1 garlic clove, minced
3 ripe tomatoes, diced
200 g (1 cup) arborio rice
   (or any other round-grain rice)
125 ml (½ cup) dry white wine

12 raw shrimp, peeled
250 g (8 oz) asparagus, blanched and
   cut in lengths
1 kg (2 lbs) lobster, cooked and peeled
1 tbsp cilantro, chopped
1 tbsp fresh parsley, minced
Sea salt
Fresh ground black pepper

In a pot, bring fish stock to a boil. Reduce heat to lowest setting and cover.

In a large saucepan, heat oil and 1 tbsp butter over medium heat. Add green onions and garlic, then cook 4 to 5 minutes without colouring, stirring from time to time.

Add tomatoes and rice, then cook around 5 minutes, stirring so rice is well coated. Pour in wine and cook while stirring non-stop until wine is fully absorbed.

Using a ladle, add 125 ml (½ cup) fish stock. Reduce heat to medium-low and continue cooking, stirring non-stop, until liquid is fully absorbed again.

Add shrimp. Pour in remaining fish stock using the same method, 125 ml (½ cup) at a time. (Overall cooking time should total around 20 minutes or until rice is cooked al dente.)

Near the very end of cooking, add asparagus and lobster along with the last ladle of fish stock and reheat while stirring gently. Remove pan from heat. Add in 1 tbsp salted butter and mix in carefully.

Season with salt and pepper. Sprinkle with cilantro and parsley, then serve.

MEAT
& POULTRY
Carnes

BEEF WITH CHOURIÇO & BEAN STEW

Carne estufada com chouriço e feijão lima

SERVES: 4
SOAKING: 12 TO 24 HOURS
PREPARATION: 30 MINUTES
COOKING: AROUND 3 HOURS

500 g (4 ½ cups) dried white beans
3 ripe tomatoes, cut into quarters
1 onion, studded with 2 cloves
2 sprigs parsley
2 sprigs thyme
2 bay leaves
2 tbsp butter
5 tbsp extra-virgin olive oil
1 kg (2 lbs) blade or shoulder roast, cut into cubes
10 pearl onions

100 g (3.5 oz) smoked lardons
1 *chouriço* (chorizo)
1 tbsp all-purpose flour
250 ml (1 cup) chicken broth
2 carrots, peeled and sliced into rounds
3 garlic cloves
2 tsp piri-piri sauce
Parsley, chopped, to taste
Sea salt
Fresh ground black pepper

The day before, in a large bowl, soak white beans in at least twice the amount of cold water, changing water once or twice.

When ready to cook, drain beans. Transfer to a large pot with tomatoes, onion, 1 sprig parsley, 1 sprig thyme and 1 bay leaf. Cover with cold water and bring to a boil. Reduce heat to medium and cook 1 hour.

Meanwhile, heat butter and oil in a Dutch oven. Add beef cubes and brown on all sides. Remove meat from Dutch oven and reserve in a plate.

In the same Dutch oven, sauté pearl onions, lardons and *chouriço* until lightly browned. Discard half the cooking fat and return meat to Dutch oven. Sprinkle with flour, stir using a wooden spoon and let brown.

Pour in chicken broth and mix. Add carrots, garlic, remaining thyme and parsley as well as second bay leaf. Bring to a boil, cover and let simmer for 1 hour over medium heat.

Drain beans (after 1 hour of cooking, they should still be a little firm) and add to meat in Dutch oven. Continue cooking for 45 minutes over medium heat.

Season with salt and add piri-piri sauce to taste. Sprinkle with chopped parsley and serve quite hot.

BAKED PORK RIBS

Entrecosto no forno

SERVINGS: 4
PREPARATION: 10 MINUTES
MARINADE: 4 HOURS
COOKING: 45 MINUTES

1 kg (2 lbs) pork ribs

MARINADE
3 garlic cloves
1 tbsp paprika
125 ml (½ cup) extra-virgin olive oil
125 ml (½ cup) white wine
3 sprigs fresh parsley, minced
1 crushed bay leaf
A few drops piri-piri sauce, to taste
1 pinch of sea salt

In a blender, purée marinade ingredients. Pour into a large resealable bag. Add meat and knead until well coated. Let marinate in refrigerator at least 4 hours.

Preheat oven to 190°C (375°F).

Remove meat from marinade and transfer to a baking dish. Reserve marinade. Cover baking dish, transfer to oven and cook meat for 45 minutes. Turn over halfway through cooking and baste with marinade.

Serve with an arugula salad, piri-piri mustard (see recipe p. 205), pickled vegetables (see recipe p. 204) and/or fried onions.

ALL-DRESSED CROQUE MONSIEUR

Francesinha

SERVINGS: 4
PREPARATION: 30 MINUTES
COOKING: 45 MINUTES

2 onions, chopped
3 garlic cloves, chopped
125 ml (½ cup) extra-virgin olive oil
2 tbsp tomato paste
125 ml (½ cup) port wine
250 ml (1 cup) pale ale
250 ml (1 cup) veal stock
1 tsp piri-piri sauce
4 tbsp all-purpose flour
6 tbsp fresh parsley, chopped
8 slices white bread
4 very thin veal scallops
4 very thin slices cooked ham
1 smoked pork sausage, sliced
    (if possible, use *linguiça*, a mini-chorizo)
8 slices São Jorge or Emmental cheese
4 eggs (optional)
Sea salt
Fresh ground black pepper

In a pan over medium heat, sauté onion and garlic in half the olive oil until golden. Add tomato paste, port wine and beer, then cook over high heat for 3 minutes. Pour in veal stock and piri-piri sauce, reduce heat to low and let simmer gently for 15 to 20 minutes.

Sprinkle with 4 tbsp flour and whip vigorously to thicken sauce.
Add chopped parsley, remove from heat and keep this port sauce warm.

Toast sliced bread.

In a large skillet over medium-high heat, cook scallops in remaining olive oil, around 3 minutes per side. Season with salt and pepper to taste. Place 1 scallop on each slice of toasted bread. Top with a slice of bread. Top with 1 slice of ham, a few slices of sausage and 1 slice of cheese. Close sandwiches with a third slice of bread, then top with cheese.

Serve these *francesinhas* drizzled with plenty of port sauce and capped with an egg, if desired!

CHORIZO

Chouriço

Of all the ingredients associated with Portugal, *chouriço* has to be the best known. This pork sausage, with its distinctive paprika-tinted brownish-red casing, overflows with flavour, and will be one of your best allies in exploring Portuguese cuisine. *Chouriço's* disarming simplicity works well with a piece of bread, a soup or a glass of *vinho verde*. Because *chouriço* is so versatile and tasty, you'll want to add this sausage to everything once you've discovered it!

PORK TENDERLOINS WITH PORT & BLUEBERRY SAUCE

Lombinhos de porco com molho ao porto e mertilhos

SERVINGS: 4
PREPARATION: 15 MINUTES
COOKING: 50 MINUTES

2 pork tenderloins, approx. 500 g (1 lb) each
3 tbsp extra-virgin olive oil
1 shallot, minced
250 g (2 ¼ cups) cremini mushrooms, cut into quarters
125 ml (½ cup) beef broth
125 ml (½ cup) port
2 tsp brown sugar
2 tbsp fresh rosemary
2 tbsp fresh oregano
150 g (1 cup) fresh blueberries
Sea salt
Fresh ground black pepper

In a Dutch oven, brown whole pork tenderloins in olive oil for 15 minutes, turning over from time to time. Remove from Dutch oven and reserve in a plate.

Add shallots and mushrooms to cooking juices remaining in Dutch oven and let soften for around 10 minutes. Pour in beef broth and mix well. Incorporate port and brown sugar, then let reduce for 5 minutes.

Return tenderloins to Dutch oven. Add rosemary and oregano, then season lightly with salt and pepper. Half-cover and let simmer for 15 minutes, stirring often.

Remove tenderloins from pot and cut into medium slices. Return slices to sauce, add blueberries and simmer uncovered for 5 minutes.

Serve with a two-potato gratin (see recipe p. 154).

RABBIT FRICASSEE WITH OLIVES

Coelho de fricassé com azeitonas

SERVINGS: 4
PREPARATION: 25 MINUTES
COOKING: 1 HOUR

100 g (3.5 oz) smoked lardons, diced
4 saddles of rabbit (see note)
2 medium onions, chopped
3 shallots, chopped
1 garlic clove, chopped
250 ml (1 cup) dry white wine
250 ml (1 cup) chicken broth
1 bouquet garni
½ tsp ground nutmeg
200 g (2 cups) mushrooms, cut into quarters
1 tbsp butter
1 tbsp flour
4 egg yolks
2 tbsp lemon juice
2 tbsp black olives (with or without pits)
1 tbsp parsley, chopped
Sea salt
Fresh ground black pepper

NOTE
You can replace the rabbit with any fowl of your choice.

In a Dutch oven, cook diced lardons over medium heat until they render their fat. Add rabbit saddles and brown gently to prevent the fat from burning.

Add onions, shallots and garlic. Once they start releasing their aromas (around 5 minutes), pour in white wine and chicken broth. Add bouquet garni, nutmeg, salt and pepper.

Bring to a boil, reduce heat, cover and let simmer for 30 minutes.

Add mushrooms and cook very slowly for 10 more minutes.

When ready to serve, in a bowl, combine butter, flour, egg yolks, lemon juice and olives. Remove Dutch oven from heat and add this mixture to the sauce in 3 to 4 instalments, whipping after each addition. Return Dutch oven to heat, bring to a boil again and let boil for a scant 2 minutes to blend well.

Sprinkle with chopped parsley. Serve with rice or home fries.

LAMB SHANKS IN RED WINE

Pernil de borrego com vinho tinto

SERVES: 4
PREPARATION: 20 MINUTES
COOKING: 4 HOURS

4 lamb shanks
4 tbsp butter
2 tsp mustard seeds
2 carrots, peeled and diced
1 red bell pepper, diced
2 onions, chopped
1 tbsp unbleached all-purpose flour
2 tbsp Dijon mustard
250 ml (1 cup) red wine
250 ml (1 cup) chicken broth
Sea salt
Fresh ground black pepper

Place rack in the middle and preheat oven to 180°C (350°F).

In a large ovenproof pot or skillet, brown shanks in half the butter, around 5 minutes on each side to brown nicely. Season with salt and pepper. Add mustard seeds and continue cooking around 2 minutes. Reserve on a plate.

In the same pot, sauté vegetables in remaining butter around 3 to 4 minutes. Season with salt and pepper. Sprinkle with flour and add Dijon mustard, mixing well. Deglaze with wine and bring to a boil while stirring. Add broth and return meat to pot. Bring to a boil once again.

Cover and braise in oven for 2 hours. Remove cover and continue cooking around 1 hour 30 minutes, or until meat detaches easily from bone, turning over shanks from time to time.

If desired, removed shanks from pot at the end of cooking and reduce sauce on the stove until thickened to a nice, syrupy consistency.

RABBIT IN MUSTARD SAUCE

Coelho com mostarda

SERVINGS: 4
PREPARATION: 25 MINUTES
COOKING: 45 MINUTES

120 g (½ cup) butter
2 tbsp whole-grain mustard
1 whole rabbit, cut in pieces
2 sprigs fresh thyme, chopped
1 sprig fresh rosemary, chopped
2 bay leaves
250 ml (1 cup) water
250 ml (1 cup) dry white wine
125 ml (½ cup) heavy (35%) whipping cream
2 tsp Dijon mustard
Thyme and rosemary, chopped, to taste (for serving)
3 tbsp parsley, chopped (for serving)
Sea salt
Fresh ground black pepper

Preheat oven to 200°C (400°F).

In a bowl, using a fork, blend together butter and whole-grain mustard. Season with salt and pepper.

Baste rabbit pieces with mustard butter, then arrange in a baking dish. Sprinkle with thyme, rosemary and bay leaves. Pour over water and white wine. Bake for 35 minutes, basting with cooking juices from time to time.

Pour cream in a small pan and bring to a boil. Remove immediately from heat, add Dijon mustard and season to taste.

Arrange rabbit pieces in a large serving platter and drizzle with sauce. Sprinkle with a little thyme, rosemary and chopped fresh parsley. Serve.

MARINATED-PORK SANDWICHES

Bifanas

SERVINGS: 4
PREPARATION: 15 MINUTES
MARINADE: 8 TO 12 HOURS
COOKING: 5 MINUTES

4 pork scallops (preferably from pork
   shoulder), around 125 g (4 oz) each
Oil (for grill)
4 country-style dinner rolls
8 slices São Jorge cheese
   (see note 3, p. 47)
Piri-piri mustard, to taste
   (see recipe p. 205)
Piri-piri sauce, to taste

MARINADE
2 tbsp lemon juice
1 to 2 garlic cloves, chopped
Piri-piri sauce, to taste
1 tbsp smoked paprika
125 ml (½ cup) white wine
60 ml (¼ cup) extra-virgin olive oil
2 bay leaves
2 tsp dried oregano
Sea salt
Fresh ground black pepper

PREPARING MARINADE

In a bowl, mix together marinade ingredients. Pour into a resealable
container, add meat and knead until well coated. Let marinate from 8 to
12 hours in refrigerator.

PREPARING SANDWICHES

Preheat barbecue on high and oil grate.

Open bread rolls in 2 and arrange them on upper grate so they can toast as
the meat cooks.

Remove meat from marinade. Arrange scallops on very hot grate and grill
for 1 to 2 minutes on each side.

Place a scallop inside each toasty dinner roll and top with 2 slices of
cheese. Brush the other half of the roll with mustard, sprinkle with a few
drops of piri-piri sauce, to taste, and close sandwich. Serve.

LAMB TARTARE

Tártaro de borrego

SERVINGS: 4
PREPARATION: 15 MINUTES

500 g (1 lb) lamb loin, finely chopped with a knife
4 shallots, chopped
1 garlic clove, chopped
3 tbsp mint leaves, minced
3 tbsp parsley, minced
4 tbsp capers
1 tsp Worcestershire sauce
1 tbsp Dijon mustard
1 tbsp lemon juice
4 egg yolks
1 tbsp green peppercorns, chopped
Piri-piri sauce, to taste
Sea salt
Fresh ground black pepper

DECORATION
1 tsp mint leaves, chopped
4 orange supremes

Combine all of the ingredients except egg yolks in a large bowl. Taste and, if needed, adjust seasoning and add piri-piri sauce to taste.

Using a large cookie cutter, mould tartare in four large pre-chilled serving plates. Place an egg yolk in the centre of each tartare. Decorate with a little chopped mint and an orange supreme.

Serve with oven-baked potatoes (see recipe p. 161).

CHICKEN SAUSAGE MEATBALLS WITH APPLES

Alheiras com maçãs

SERVINGS: 4
PREPARATION: 30 MINUTES
COOKING : 15 MINUTES

2 tbsp butter
2 apples, peeled, seeded and cut in large chunks
125 ml (½ cup) white port
Cinnamon, to taste
4 chicken sausages
2 tbsp extra-virgin olive oil
Sea salt

In a skillet, melt butter over medium heat and add apple chunks. Pour in white port and let reduce for 2 minutes. Season with salt and sprinkle with cinnamon. Remove from heat and reserve.

Preheat oven to 180°C (350°F). Line a cookie sheet with wax paper.

Remove meat from sausage casings and shape into small meatballs, around 3 cm (1 ¼ in) each. Brush meatballs with olive oil.

In a skillet, heat 1 tbsp olive oil. Add meatballs and lightly brown for 3 to 4 minutes.

Arrange port-flavoured apples on prepared cookie sheet. Top with meatballs and bake in oven for 10 minutes.

Serve this dish very hot.

MARINATED QUAILS & OVEN-ROASTED POTATOES

Codornizes no forno

SERVINGS: 4
PREPARATION: 10 MINUTES
MACERATION: 3 HOURS
COOKING: 1 HOUR

4 royal quails
2 tbsp butter
16 whole fingerling potatoes or baby potatoes
Sea salt
Fresh ground black pepper

MARINADE
6 tbsp extra-virgin olive oil
125 ml (½ cup) white wine
1 tsp piri-piri sauce
2 tbsp fresh rosemary, chopped
1 garlic clove, chopped
6 tbsp fresh parsley, chopped
1 tsp ground nutmeg (or ground cumin)
Sea salt
1 bay leaf

Start by preparing marinade. In a bowl, whisk together olive oil, white wine, piri-piri sauce, rosemary, parsley, garlic and nutmeg. Season with salt to taste. Add bay leaf.

Pour this marinade in a resealable bag and add quails. Seal bag and knead quails until well coated. Marinate in refrigerator around 3 hours.

Preheat oven to 180°C (350°F).

In an ovenproof dish, combine butter, quails and their marinade. Add potatoes, then season with salt and pepper. Bake in oven for 1 hour.

Remove from oven. Place 1 quail and 4 potatoes in each dinner plate. Serve with squash spaghetti or confit tomatoes (see recipes pp. 150 and 168).

CHICKEN À BRAZ

Frango, camarão e chouriço à braz

SERVINGS: 4
PREPARATION: 25 MINUTES
COOKING: 20 MINUTES

1 onion, cut in 2 then sliced
3 garlic cloves, chopped
200 g (1 ¾ cups) *chouriço* (chorizo), diced
225 g (8 oz) your choice of mushrooms
3 tbsp extra-virgin olive oil
250 ml (1 cup) chicken broth
500 g (3 ¾ cups) chicken breasts, cooked and cut into
    chunks
1 bay leaf
500 g (1 lb) medium-size shrimp, peeled
6 eggs, lightly beaten
Parsley, chopped, to taste
A few olives, to taste (for serving)
Sea salt
Fresh ground black pepper

SHOESTRING FRIES
Vegetable oil (for frying)
500 g (3 cups) potatoes, very finely julienned

PREPARING SHOESTRING FRIES
In a deep fryer, preheat enough vegetable oil to 180°C (350°F). Add potatoes to hot oil and fry until golden-crisp. Remove fries from oil and reserve on paper towels.

In a pan, sauté onion, garlic, *chouriço* and mushrooms in olive oil until golden brown.

Deglaze with chicken broth. Add chicken pieces and mix. Season with salt, pepper and bay leaf, then simmer for a few minutes. Add shrimp and shoestring fries, mixing well. Incorporate beaten eggs and parsley, stirring non-stop.

Divide preparation among four dinner plates. Garnish with a few olives and serve with a salad.

CORNISH HEN & CLAMS

Frango com ameijoas

SERVINGS: 4
PREPARATION: 30 MINUTES
MARINADE: 60 MINUTES
COOKING: 50 MINUTES

1 whole chicken, cut into 4 pieces
Coarse salt
Juice of ½ lemon
3 garlic cloves, chopped
1 tbsp smoked paprika
60 ml (¼ cup) extra-virgin olive oil
250 ml (1 cup) chicken broth,
   or more as needed
125 ml (½ cup) dry white wine
3 bay leaves
Piri-piri sauce or other hot sauce,
   to taste

4 Italian tomatoes, diced
500 g (1 lb) choice of root vegetables
   (carrots, celeriac, small potatoes,
   etc.), or squash, peeled and cut to
   the same size
3 to 4 tbsp flat-leaf parsley, fresh thyme
   or rosemary (leaves only), chopped
16 clams
1 dash extra-virgin olive oil (for serving)

Preheat oven to 200°C (400°F).

Rub chicken pieces with coarse salt. Place in a large dish, sprinkle with a little lemon juice. Cover and let rest in refrigerator for 60 minutes.

In a bowl, mix garlic, smoked paprika, olive oil, chicken broth, white wine, bay leaves and piri-piri sauce.

In a large baking dish, arrange tomatoes, root vegetables and chicken pieces. Add in flavoured broth and your choice of fresh herb, then mix so that vegetables and chicken are well coated.

Arrange chicken pieces on top, skin side up. Bake in oven for 45 to 50 minutes or until flesh is cooked and skin is golden brown. Check the quantity of liquid halfway through and drizzle with chicken broth a few times.

Around 10 minutes before the end of cooking, add clams and a little chicken broth, if needed. Once clams open, remove dish from oven. (Discard unopened clams.)

Transfer food to a serving platter and drizzle with a little olive oil. Serve very hot.

SIDES
Acompanhamentos

PORTUGUESE BLOOD PUDDING WITH RICE

Morcela de arroz

SERVINGS: 4
PREPARATION: 45 MINUTES
COOKING: 40MINUTES

2 onions, minced
2 tsp extra-virgin olive oil
1 kg (2 lbs) marinated pork, diced in small cubes
   (see recipe p. 134)
1 L (4 cups) water
200 g (1 cup) long-grain rice
1 tsp ground cloves
1 tbsp ground cumin
1 tbsp smoked paprika
2 tbsp parsley, chopped
125 ml (½ cup) pig blood (see note)
Natural hog casings (see note)

NOTE
Pig blood and natural hog casings can be found in Portuguese butcher shops (see Good Addresses p. 209).

In a Dutch oven, sauté onions in olive oil over medium heat. Add diced pork and brown on all sides for 5 minutes. Pour in the water, add rice and continue cooking around 10 minutes. Remove Dutch oven from heat. Season with cloves, cumin and smoked paprika. Mix, then let cool.

Once preparation is lukewarm, add in parsley and pig blood, mixing well.

Knot each casing at one end, then fill with mixture using a funnel. Make sure there's enough liquid inside so that the rice can continue cooking and swelling. If needed, add a little water. Knot the other end.

Half-fill a large pot with water and bring to a boil. Add blood puddings and cook around 15 minutes, pricking each casing with a needle (or fork) to drain out excess liquid.

Remove blood puddings from the pot. Serve with tomato jam on the side (see recipe p. 200).

SPAGHETTI SQUASH WITH TOMATO & FRESH CHEESE

Abóbora com tomates e queijo fresco

SERVINGS: 4
PREPARATION: 15 MINUTES
COOKING: 50 MINUTES

1 spaghetti squash, approx. 1.5 kg (3 lbs)
60 ml (¼ cup) extra-virgin olive oil
2 medium onions, minced
1 garlic clove, fminced
125 ml (½ cup) chicken broth
300 g (2 cups) whole cherry tomatoes
4 tbsp black olives, pitted and minced
150 g (¾ cup) fresh cheese, diced (see recipe p. 201)
4 tbsp fresh parsley, chopped
Sea salt
Fresh ground black pepper

Preheat oven to 200°C (400°F). Line a cooking sheet with parchment paper.

Cut squash in 2 lengthwise and remove seeds. Season with salt and pepper. Place both squash halves on prepared cooking sheet, cut side down. Bake in oven for 45 minutes or until flesh is tender to the point of a knife. Remove from oven and let cool slightly.

Shred squash flesh using a fork and transfer to a bowl. Add 3 tbsp olive oil, season with salt and pepper, then keep warm.

In a skillet over medium heat, brown onions in remaining oil around 4 to 5 minutes. Season with salt and pepper. Add garlic and cook for 1 minute. Mix in broth, cherry tomatoes and olives. Cover and let simmer around 5 minutes or until tomatoes burst slightly. Remove from heat. Add cheese and adjust seasoning.

Serve this sauce on a bed of spaghetti squash and sprinkle with fresh parsley.

CREAM OF GREEN PEA SOUP WITH *CHOURIÇO* CHIPS

Creme de ervilhas e frituras de chouriço

SERVINGS: 4
PREPARATION: 20 MINUTES
COOKING: 25 MINUTES

1 leek, minced
1 potato, peeled and cut in large cubes
2 tbsp butter
2 tbsp extra-virgin olive oil
1 L (4 cups) chicken broth
500 g (1 lbs) frozen green peas
1 *chouriço* (chorizo), sliced into rounds
30 g (¾ cup) fresh mint, minced
Sea salt
Fresh ground black pepper

TOPPINGS
Chouriço chips (see recipe p. 199)

NOTE
This soup will be just as delicious served hot or cold, as a starter. You may prepare it 2 or 3 hours ahead of time and chill it in the refrigerator. Make sure you cover and seal it with plastic wrap so it doesn't dry. For a hearty version, add 500 g (1 lb) cooked and shredded crabmeat, divided between soup bowls right before serving.

In a pot, sauté leek and potato in butter and olive oil for 5 minutes over medium heat.

Pour in chicken broth and season. Bring to a boil, reduce heat to low and simmer uncovered for 10 minutes or until potatoes are very tender.

Add in green peas and *chouriço*, then continue cooking for 5 minutes. Remove from heat and let cool a few minutes. Add fresh mint. Transfer to a blender and purée until smooth.

TWO-POTATO GRATIN

Gratinado de batatas

SERVINGS: 4
PREPARATION: 30 MINUTES
COOKING: 40 MINUTES

Oil (for dish)
2 large Yukon Gold potatoes, peeled and thinly sliced
2 tsp garlic, chopped
1 tbsp thyme, chopped
1 tbsp cilantro, chopped
3 tbsp extra-virgin olive oil
2 sweet potatoes, peeled and thinly sliced
375 ml (1 ½ cups) chicken broth
Sea salt
Fresh ground pepper

TOPPINGS
100 g (1 cup) corn bread, torn into small pieces
    (see recipe p. 158)
1 tsp garlic, chopped
100 g (1 cup) São Jorge cheese, grated (see note)
2 tbsp olive oil

NOTE
You can replace São Jorge with the same amount of your favourite cheese.

Preheat oven to 180 °C (350 °F).

Oil a large baking dish. Arrange half the sliced potatoes in a single layer. Sprinkle with half the garlic, thyme and cilantro. Season with salt and pepper, then drizzle with olive oil.

Arrange sweet potato slices over first layer, then sprinkle with remaining garlic, thyme and cilantro. Season with salt and pepper, then drizzle once again with olive oil. Add remaining sliced potatoes in a final layer and brush with olive oil.

Reheat chicken broth in microwave or in a pan on the stove. Pour hot broth over potatoes. (The top layer should be barely covered.) Bake 25 minutes.

PREPARING TOPPINGS
Meanwhile, in a bowl, combine torn bread with garlic, grated cheese and olive oil. Season with salt and pepper. Sprinkle over potatoes and return to oven for 15 minutes or until potatoes are tender and cheese golden brown.

SWEET POTATO MIGAS

Gratinado de batatas

SERVINGS: 4
PREPARATION: 15 MINUTES
COOKING: 25 MINUTES

3 garlic cloves, minced
125 ml (½ cup) extra-virgin olive oil + 1 dash for dressing
2 tsp chili powder
Around 900 g (6 cups) sweet potatoes,
    peeled and quartered
30 g (½ cup) kale
100 g (1 cup) crustless corn bread, diced very small
    (see receipt p.158)
2 tbsp red wine vinegar
6 tbsp cilantro, chopped
Sea salt
Fresh ground pepper

Preheat oven to 230°C (450°F). Line a cooking sheet with parchment paper.

In a large bowl, combine garlic, oil and chili powder. Generously season with salt and pepper. Add potato wedges and mix with your hands until well coated with oil. Arrange potatoes on the cooking sheet and bake in oven for 20 minutes. Turn over potatoes and continue baking for 5 minutes or until tender. Remove from oven and let cool slightly.

Meanwhile, in a pot of boiling water, blanch kale leaves for 1 minute. Drain and transfer to a bowl of cold water to stop the cooking. Drain kale again and expel excess water with your hands. Finely chop and transfer to a large bowl. Add in cooled sweet potatoes and diced bread. Drizzle with olive oil and vinegar, then sprinkle with chopped cilantro.

An excellent side for fish or roasted meats!

CORNBREAD

Pão de milho

YIELD: 4 LOAVES
PREPARATION: 20 MINUTES
RESTING: 2 HOURS
COOKING: 1 HOUR

1 kg (7 ½ cups) yellow corn flour
500 g (4 cups) wheat flour
16.5 g (1 ½ pouch) baker's yeast
1 L (4 cups) water
150 g (½ cup) sourdough starter (see note 1)
1 tsp salt

NOTES

1. *To prepare sourdough, combine 125 ml (½ cup) boiling water and 75 g (2.5 oz) yeast. Add around 30 g (¼ cup) flour and a pinch of salt, then mix and let rest overnight in a cool place so the bread can rise into an even shape. In all, dough should double in size.*
2. *You may slice and freeze this bread to keep some on hand at all times. Since cornbread is best enjoyed warm, simply reheat before serving.*

Preheat oven to 240°C (475°F).

Sift corn flour over a large bowl. Add wheat flour and yeast, mixing well.

Heat water in a pan without bringing to a boil.

Add flours to hot water, a little at a time, kneading as you go. Incorporate sourdough and knead until dough becomes smooth and elastic. Shape dough into a ball. Cover with a cloth and let rise for 2 hours or so in a warm place away from drafts.

Divide dough in 4 equally-sized balls and arrange on a lightly floured cooking sheet. Bake in oven for 10 minutes.

Reduce oven temperature to 220°C (425°F) and bake for 45 minutes more, glancing in from time to time until crust turns golden brown.

Remove from oven and let cool on a rack.

OVEN-BAKED POTATOES

Batatinhas no forno

SERVINGS: 4
PREPARATION: 10 MINUTES
COOKING: 1 HOUR 15 MINUTES

1 kg (2 lbs) whole fingerling potatoes (or baby potatoes)
60 ml (¼ cup) extra-virgin olive oil
2 tbsp duck fat
3 garlic cloves, cut in 2
2 sprigs fresh rosemary
2 sprigs fresh thyme
3 tbsp fresh parsley, chopped
Fleur de sel
Fresh ground black pepper

Preheat oven to 180°C (350°F) and place rack in the middle.

In a large ovenproof dish, mix all the ingredients. Bake in oven for 1 hour 15 minutes, stirring often during cooking.

OVEN-BAKED STUFFED POTATOES

Batatas recheadas

SERVINGS: 6
PREPARATION: 20 MINUTES
COOKING: 25 MINUTES

12 medium potatoes, each cut in 2
3 tbsp extra-virgin olive oil
Chives, chopped (for garnish)
Dill, chopped (for garnish)

STUFFING
100 g (3.5 oz) smoked salmon, finely chopped
1 can (125 g/4 oz) sardines in olive oil
2 tbsp heavy (35%) cream
1 tsp lemon juice
2 tbsp capers, drained and chopped
2 tbsp red onion, minced
½ tsp horseradish powder
Sea salt
Fresh ground black pepper

Preheat oven to 180°C (350°F). Line a cooking sheet with parchment paper.

Remove a thin slice under all potato halves to prevent wobbling. Place potatoes in a bowl, sprinkle with olive oil and mix well.

Arrange potatoes on the cooking sheet, cut side down. Bake in oven for 25 minutes or until tender.

Meanwhile, prepare stuffing. In a bowl, combine smoked salmon, sardines, cream, lemon juice, capers, onion and horseradish. Season with salt and pepper.

Scoop out potato flesh to create a cavity, taking care not to pierce the peel. Add potato flesh to stuffing and mix.

Place 1 tbsp stuffing in each potato. Sprinkle with chopped chives and dill, then serve.

SÃO JORGE CHEESE SHORTBREADS
WITH *CHOURIÇO* & OLIVES

Ariados de queijo, chouriço e azeitonas

YIELD: 12 SHORTBREADS
PREPARATION: 10 MINUTES
REFRIGERATION: 45 MINUTES
COOKING: 15 MINUTES

140 g (1 cup) all-purpose flour
60 g (¼ cup) butter, softened
1 tsp sea salt
6 tbsp water
½ *chouriço* (chorizo), diced
50 g (½ cup) São Jorge cheese (or another hard cheese
    of your choice), grated
75 g (½ cup) pitted black olives

NOTE
*Let shortbreads cool
in cooking sheet because they are
very fragile while hot.*

In a large bowl, using fingertips, combine flour, butter and salt.
Add water and mix until the dough is smooth and homogeneous.
Add diced *chouriço*, cheese and olives, then mix well.

On a floured work surface, fashion the dough into a log and wrap in
plastic wrap. Chill around 45 minutes in refrigerator.

Preheat oven to 180°C (350°F). Line a cooking sheet with parchment
paper.

Cut dough log in 12 slices and arrange on prepared cooking sheet. Bake
shortbreads around 15 minutes or until golden.

OLIVE OIL

Azeite

This typically Mediterranean marvel
is the gold standard, as unique as each family that
produces it. In Portuguese culture, the know-how
for creating the perfect olive oil is passed on from
father to son and mother to daughter.
Each bottle ends up containing a flavourful
memory that resists the passage of time.
This is why it's important for me to share this
family treasure with you, by making a few bottles
of my personal vintage available in my
restaurants and boutiques.

CONFIT CHERRY TOMATOES

Tomates confitados

SERVINGS: 4
PREPARATION: 10 MINUTES
COOKING: 25 MINUTES

300 g (2 cups) cherry tomatoes, cut in 2
3 tbsp extra-virgin olive oil
1 tsp sugar
3 garlic cloves, sliced paper-thin
1 tbsp dried oregano
Sea salt
Fresh ground black pepper

NOTE
Confit tomatoes are a perfect side for grilled sardine fillets, cod or other roasted fish.

Preheat oven to 200°C (400°F). Line a cooking sheet with parchment paper, then lightly oil the paper.

Place tomato halves on cooking sheet, cut side down. Drizzle with oil, season with salt and pepper, then sprinkle with sugar.

Place a garlic wafer on all tomato halves and bake in oven around 25 minutes or until they start to caramelize and collapse.

When serving, sprinkle with dried oregano.

EGGPLANT CAVIAR-STUFFED TOMATOES

Tomates recheados com beringelas

SERVINGS: 4
PREPARATION: 15 MINUTES
COOKING: 45 MINUTES

2 eggplants, approx. 400 g (14 oz) each, cut in 2
8 confit garlic cloves (see note)
1 tsp flat-leaf parsley, minced
½ tsp lemon juice
8 medium tomatoes
50 g (½ cup) hard cheese (São Jorge, aged cheddar
    or Emmental), grated
8 eggs
Sea salt
Fresh ground black pepper

NOTE
To confit garlic, in a small pan, bring to a boil 3 tbsp garlic oil with 8 garlic cloves, peeled, cut in 2 and germ removed. Reduce to lowest heat and let simmer gently for 20 minutes. Remove from oven and set aside.

Preheat oven to 180°C (350°F). Line a cooking sheet with parchment paper.

Place eggplants on cooking sheet, cut side down. Bake in middle of the oven around 30 minutes. Remove from oven and let cool slightly. Keep oven on.

With a spoon, scoop out eggplant flesh and transfer to a sieve. Let drain for 2 to 3 minutes.

In a food processor, purée 200 g (2 cups) eggplant flesh with confit garlic, parsley and lemon juice. Season this caviar with salt and pepper.

Remove tops from tomatoes and scoop out their flesh using a small melon baller (or small spoon), taking care not to break the skin. Stuff tomatoes with eggplant caviar.

Top tomatoes with grated cheese, then break a whole egg in the middle of each one. Bake in oven for 15 minutes, at 180°C (350°F).

Serve as a side for grilled seafood.

DESSERTS
Sobremesas

SUGAR DOUGHNUTS

Farturas

YIELD: AROUND 30 DOUGHNUTS
PREPARATION: 15 MINUTES
COOKING: 30 MINUTES

500 ml (2 cups) milk
2 tbsp sugar
Zest of 2 limes
225 g (1 cup) unsalted butter
375 g (3 ¼ cups) all-purpose flour
8 eggs
500 ml (2 cups) vegetable oil (for frying)
55 g (¼ cup) sugar

NOTE
This batter freezes quite well. Arrange dough logs on a cooking sheet lined with parchment paper instead of frying them. Place the cooking sheet in the freezer, then transfer frozen farturas into a freezer bag. They will keep for up to 1 month. They don't need to be thawed before frying.

In a large pan, bring to a boil milk, sugar, lime zest and butter. Once mixture is boiling, remove pan from heat and add flour all at once. Mix with a wooden spoon until flour is fully absorbed. Return pan to heat and cook 2 minutes while stirring non-stop.

Pour batter in a bowl and add in eggs one by one, mixing with the wooden spoon between each addition.

Transfer batter to a pastry bag fitted with a fluted tip.

Preheat deep fryer to 160°C (320°F) or heat oil in a large heavy-bottom skillet. Spread sugar in a small plate.

Above the fryer, shape dough into logs, 10-cm (4-in) long, letting them fall carefully into the hot oil and cutting them with scissors as you go. Fry one or two doughnuts at a time for 3 to 4 minutes or until golden. Remove from oil, letting them drain for a few seconds, then roll in the sugar. Enjoy while still hot.

BERLIN BALLS

Bolas de Berlim

YIELD: 24 DOUGHNUTS
PREPARATION: 20 MINUTES
RESTING: 1 HOUR
COOKING: 15 MINUTES

Flour (for cooking sheet and work
    surface)
5 tsp instant yeast
160 ml (⅔ cup) lukewarm water
500 g (3 ½ cups) all-purpose flour
50 g (¼ cup) sugar
2 tsp salt
4 eggs
130 g (½ cup) unsalted butter, softened
1 L (4 cups) vegetable oil (for frying)

PASTRY CREAM
100 g (½ cup) sugar
2 eggs
45 g (¾ cup) cornstarch
500 ml (2 cups) milk
1 tsp vanilla extract or ½ vanilla bean,
    split and scraped

In a small bowl, activate yeast in lukewarm water for 5 minutes.

In a food processor, combine flour, sugar, salt and eggs. Add yeast with its soaking water and mix using hook around 10 minutes (or knead by hand). Dough should be smooth and no longer sticking to the sides of the bowl.

Add soft butter and mix around 2 minutes more or until butter is well blended in.

Remove hook and cover bowl with a cloth. Let stand for 30 minutes at room temperature.

Flour a cooking sheet and work surface.

Place dough on work surface and roll out to a 2.5-cm (1-in) thickness. Cut dough in 24 small circles, 2-cm (¾-in) wide, using a small cookie cutter.

Arrange dough balls spaced apart on the floured cooking sheet. Cover sheet with a cloth and let stand for 30 minutes at room temperature.

Preheat a deep fryer to 160°C (320°F) or heat vegetable oil in a large heavy-bottom skillet. When oil is hot, add a few dough balls and fry around 2 minutes per side. Remove fried dough using a slotted spoon and transfer to a large plate lined with paper towels. Repeat until all dough is used. Let cool.

PREPARING PASTRY CREAM

Whisk sugar and eggs in a bowl until mixture whitens. Add in cornstarch and whisk again to avoid lumps. Set aside.

Over medium-high heat, warm milk and vanilla in a pan while stirring often. Once milk is boiling, add sugar-egg mixture and whip vigorously. Cook around 2 minutes. Once preparation starts to boil again, remove from heat and pour in a bowl. Cover with plastic wrap placed directly on the surface of the hot cream to avoid a skin forming and chill completely in refrigerator.

Cut each fried doughnut in 2 and fill with pastry cream. Dig in!

FIELDBERRY CRÈME BRÛLÉE

Leite creme com frutos silvestres

SERVINGS: 4
PREPARATION: 15 MINUTES
COOKING: 10 MINUTES
REFRIGERATION: 2 HOURS

5 egg yolks
6 tbsp sugar
1 tsp vanilla extract
5 tbsp cornstarch
625 ml (2 ½ cups) milk
1 cinnamon stick
Zest of ½ lemon
Zest of ½ orange
100 g (1 cup) your choice of fieldberries (blueberries,
    raspberries, blackberries, strawberries)
3 tbsp sugar

In a bowl, whisk together egg yolks, sugar and vanilla extract. Gently add in cornstarch and mix. Reserve.

In a saucepan, combine milk, cinnamon and citrus zests. Bring to a boil, then remove immediately from heat and let cool for a few minutes. Strain through a fine sieve to remove cinnamon and zests.

Return strained milk to saucepan, add egg mixture and whisk until well blended. Warm over medium heat for 2 to 3 minutes taking care not to let it boil, whisking non-stop with a whip.

Divide berries among four small ramekins, preferably clay. Pour cream over fruit without stirring to avoid the fruit staining the cream. Place ramekins in refrigerator and let cool completely.

To serve, sprinkle ramekins with sugar and caramelize using a kitchen blowtorch or broiling in oven.

HEAVENLY CREAM

Natas de céu

SERVINGS: 12
PREPARATION: 15 MINUTES
COOKING: 5 MINUTES

CREAM
250 ml (1 cup) heavy (35%) whipping cream
200 g (1 cup) sugar
4 egg whites
½ package Maria cookies (Graham-style cookies),
    crumbled

EGG YOLK SYRUP
250 g (1 ¼ cups) sugar
60 ml (¼ sugar) water
10 egg yolks

PREPARING CREAM

In a bowl (preferably well chilled), whip heavy cream until semi-firm peaks form. Cover with plastic wrap laid directly on the cream and chill in refrigerator.

Pour sugar and egg whites in a pan and heat over low heat, stirring non-stop, until sugar has dissolved and a thermometer indicates 60°C (140°F). Remove from heat and whip to firm peaks.

Gradually add this whipped cream to meringue, folding in carefully using a spatula. Set aside.

PREPARING EGG YOLK SYRUP

In a pan, bring sugar and water to a boil, stirring to fully dissolve sugar, then boil around 2 minutes. Remove from heat and let cool.

Beat egg yolks in a large bowl. Pour sugared water on egg yolks and whip into a smooth syrup. Let fully cool.

ASSEMBLY

Arrange half the Maria cookies at the bottom of 12 glasses. Half-fill glasses with cream. Cover with remaining crumbled cookies. Top with remaining cream, leaving enough space to garnish with syrup. Divide egg yolk syrup among glasses and enjoy.

MERINGUE & CHOCOLATE MOUSSE DOMES

Suspiro com chocolate e calda de frutas

SERVINGS: 12
PREPARATION: 1 HOUR
FREEZING: 2 HOURS
COOKING: 2 HOURS

MERINGUES
300 g (1 ½ cups) sugar
5 egg whites

CHOCOLATE MOUSSE
1 L (4 cups) heavy (35%) whipping cream
6 egg yolks

190 ml (¾ cup) corn syrup
375 g (3 cups) 65% dark chocolate
  pistoles

GARNISH
Seasonal fruits, cut in small bites

PREPARING MERINGUES

Preheat oven to 200°C (400°F). Combine sugar and egg whites in a pan. Cook over medium heat, whisking non-stop with a whip, around 4 minutes or until candy thermometer reaches 60°C (140°F).The sugar must be completely dissolved.

Pour mixture into food processor (or use an electric mixer) and whip at maximum speed for 5 to 10 minutes or until fully cooled.

Using a spatula or spoon, fill 12 silicone moulds shaped like half-spheres with meringue. With the back of the spoon, indent middle slightly to make cooking easier. Bake in oven around 1 hour 30 minutes.

Remove meringues from oven and let stand until fully cooled before unmoulding.

PREPARING CHOCOLATE MOUSSE

Whip cream until firm but still a little liquid. Set aside in refrigerator.

Place egg yolks in a stainless-steel bowl.

In a pan, bring corn syrup to a boil. Pour this boiling syrup on egg yolks all the while whipping.

Fill a large pan with water to create a double boiler and heat until water simmers.

Place bowl with egg yolk and corn syrup mixture on top of pan of simmering water (the bowl must not touch the water) and cook while whisking non-stop for 2 minutes. Remove bowl from pan and set aside.

Place chocolate in another stainless-steel bowl. Bring the pan of water back to a gentle boil. Place bowl on top of the pan (without coming in contact with water) to melt chocolate. Once chocolate is fully melted, add the egg yolk mixture and whip, using a whip or electric mixer, until homogeneous.

Add semi-firm cream in three instalments, whipping between each one.

Using a spatula or spoon, fill 12 silicone moulds shaped like half-spheres with mousse, leaving a slight hollow in the middle. Place moulds on a cookie sheet and wrap in plastic wrap. Freeze for 2 hours.

Remove moulds from freezer and unmould. Place half-spheres of meringue on serving plates and fill cavities with seasonal fruits. Place half-spheres of chocolate mousse on top to form domes. Enjoy!

ANGEL FOOD CAKE

Pão de lo de ovar

SERVINGS: 10
PREPARATION: 10 MINUTES
COOKING: 35 MINUTES

Butter (for the cake pan)
11 egg yolks
2 whole eggs
1 tsp salt
200 g (1 cups) sugar
70 g (½ cup) all-purpose flour
1 tsp baking powder

Preheat oven to 180°C (350°F).

Butter a 22-cm (9-in) round cake pan. Line pan with a sheet of waxed paper, then butter paper.

In a large bowl, beat egg yolks with whole eggs, salt and sugar, using an electric mixer, for a few minutes until foamy.

In another bowl, combine flour and baking powder. Using a spatula, gently fold into the beaten eggs. (Important: Do not fold in using electric mixer.)

Pour batter into the prepared cake pan. Bake around 35 minutes. Check for doneness by inserting a wooden toothpick towards the outer edge of cake and not its centre, which must remain very moist. Once toothpick comes out clean, remove cake from oven and let cool in the pan before unmoulding.

ORANGE-THYME POUND CAKE

Bolo de laranja

SERVINGS: 12
PREPARATION: 30 MINUTES
COOKING: 35 MINUTES

Butter (for cake pan)
300 g (2 cups) all-purpose flour
1 tbsp baking powder
1 pinch salt
300 g (1 ½ cups) sugar
300 g (1 ⅓ cups) unsalted butter, at
    room temperature
2 sprigs fresh thyme, leaves removed
Zest of 3 oranges
6 eggs

ORANGE-THYME SYRUP
Juice of 1 orange
50 g (¼ cup) sugar
1 sprig fresh thyme, leaves removed

DECORATION
Juice of 1 orange
120 g (1 cup) icing sugar + more for
    decoration (if desired)
1 orange, sliced

NOTE
*Do not refrigerate this cake
to preserve its moistness. Cover it
and keep it at room temperature
for up to 5 days. You can also freeze
it, wrapped in parchment paper,
then plastic wrap.*

Preheat oven to 180°C (350°F). Butter a Bundt cake pan.

PREPARING CAKE

In a bowl, mix flour, baking powder and salt. Set aside.

With an electric mixer or food processor, mix sugar, butter, thyme leaves and orange zest until creamy. Scrape the bottom of the bowl with a spatula. Incorporate eggs one by one, mixing between each addition and scraping the bottom of the bowl from time to time to prevent lumps forming. Once done, gradually incorporate dry ingredients.

Pour batter into prepared cake pan. Bake in oven for 30 to 40 minutes, or until a toothpick inserted in the middle comes out clean.

Meanwhile, prepare orange syrup. In a small pan, bring to a boil orange juice with icing sugar and thyme. Remove pan from heat the moment the syrup starts to boil.

Remove cake from oven. With a pastry brush, soak cake with syrup. Let cool completely before unmoulding.

DECORATING CAKE

In a small pan, boil orange juice and icing sugar while stirring, until sugar dissolves. Remove pan from heat and let preparation stand for 2 minutes before pouring it on unmoulded cake.

Arrange orange slices on top of cake. Sprinkle with icing sugar (if desired).

MARIA COOKIE PIE

Tarte de bolacha Maria

SERVINGS: 12
PREPARATION: 10 MINUTES
COOKING: 5 MINUTES
REFRIGERATION: 3 HOURS

Butter (for pie plate)
Flour (for pie plate)
250 ml (1 cup) warm espresso (see note)
3 egg yolks
75 g (¾ cup) sugar
250 ml (1 cup) milk
250 ml (1 cup) heavy (35%) whipping cream
300 g (1 ¾ cups) 75% dark chocolate, chopped
2 packages Maria cookies (Graham-style cookies)

NOTE
*If you prefer,
you can replace espresso
with warm chocolate milk.*

Butter and flour a 23-cm (9-in) pie plate.

Prepare espresso coffee and let cool.

Meanwhile, in a bowl, beat egg yolks and sugar. Reserve.

In a saucepan, heat milk and cream over low heat. Add in sugared egg yolks and mix. Remove from heat as soon as the mixture is hot and that is thickened slightly. Let cool for a few minutes.

Place chocolate previously melted in a food processor and pour in mixture. Process to a smooth chocolate cream.

Dip cookies in lukewarm coffee and arrange in a single layer over the bottom of the prepared pie plate. Cover cookies with chocolate cream. Add a second layer of cookies and cover again with chocolate cream.

Chill in refrigerator for 3 hours or so before serving.

PEAR-ALMOND PIE

Tarte de pêra e amêndoa

SERVINGS: 10
PREPARATION: 30 MINUTES
REFRIGERATION: 30 MINUTES
COOKING: 50 MINUTES

1 L (4 cups) water
200 g (1 cup) sugar
1 vanilla bean, cut in 2 lengthwise and scraped
4 firm but ripe pears, peeled and cut into quarters (see note)

SHORTBREAD CRUST (SEE NOTE)
250 g (1 ¾ cups) all-purpose flour
1 pinch of salt
150 g (⅔ cup) chilled unsalted butter, small diced

100 g (½ cup) sugar
1 egg, beaten
1 tsp vanilla extract
A few drops of cold water
Butter (for pie plate)

ALMOND CREAM
100 g (½ cup) unsalted butter, softened
100 g (½ cup) sugar
150 g (1 ¼ cup) almond powder
2 eggs
1 tsp bitter almond extract

NOTE
To save time, you can buy your shortbread pastry dough and use canned peaches.

COOKING PEARS

Pour water into a large pot. Add sugar, vanilla bean and seeds, then bring to a boil. Let reduce by half.

Carefully place pear sections into this syrup and cook over medium heat for 10 minutes. Remove from heat and let pears cool down in syrup.

PREPARING SHORTBREAD CRUST

Sift flour and salt over a clean work surface, then mound the flour and make a well in the centre. Place chilled diced butter in this well and knead with your fingers to obtain a sandy, crumbly texture.

Form dough into a ball, then push down the middle to make a new well. Add in sugar, egg, vanilla extract and a few drops of cold water. Mix with your fingertips. Roll dough into a ball and wrap in plastic wrap. Chill in refrigerator for 30 minutes.

Preheat oven to 180°C (350°F). Lightly butter a 30-cm (12-in) pie plate.

Remove dough from refrigerator, roll dough to a 1 cm (¾ in) thickness and press into the bottom and sides of the pie plate. Pinch crust edge using your fingers and prick the bottom with a fork.

PREPARING ALMOND CREAM

In a bowl, combine softened butter and sugar. Whip with an electric mixer until mixture is homogeneous. Add almond powder and bitter almond extract, then beat a little more to blend in.

Fill crust with almond cream three-quarters of the way up, then top with pear sections previously sliced crosswise. Let the pie chill in refrigerator for 30 minutes. Bake around 40 minutes or until crust turns golden.

Serve pie hot, lukewarm or cold.

MILK TARTS

Queijadas de leite

SERVINGS: 12
PREPARATION: 10 MINUTES
COOKING: 35 MINUTES

Butter (for moulds)
2 eggs
50 g (¼ cup) unsalted butter
200 g (1 cup) sugar
140 g (1 cup) all-purpose flour
500 ml (2 cups) milk
Icing sugar (for serving)
Ground cinnamon (for serving)

Preheat oven to 180°C (350°F). Butter muffin moulds.

In the food processor, beat eggs, butter and sugar for 3 minutes. Add in flour and milk, then process again for 1 minute. Carry out this step by hand, if desired.

Divide mixture among muffin moulds and bake around 35 minutes or until a toothpick inserted in the middle comes out clean.

Remove from oven and let cool before unmoulding. Sprinkle with icing sugar and cinnamon. Serve tarts lukewarm or cold.

PORTUGUESE MAPLE TARTS

Pasteis de nata com xarope de ácer

YIELD: 12 TARTS
PREPARATION: 30 MINUTES
RESTING: 4 TO 8 HOURS
COOKING: 15 MINUTES

Flour (for work surface)
250 g (8 oz) puff pastry, homemade or store-bought
375 ml (1 ½ cups) milk
6 egg yolks
2 tsp all-purpose flour
100 g (½ cup) sugar
2 tbsp maple syrup
1 cinnamon stick
Berries (blueberries, strawberries, raspberries) (optional)
Ground cinnamon, to taste

Flour work surface. With a rolling pin, roll out puff pastry as finely as possible, then roll back on itself to form a large full cylinder. Cut into rounds, 2.5-cm (1-in) wide.

In muffin moulds, place a round of dough in each cavity. With slightly wet fingers, press on dough so it lines the bottom and goes up the sides evenly. Let stand at room temperature for 4 to 8 hours, so dough won't puff up during cooking and remain very flaky.

Preheat oven to 230°C (450°F).

Pour milk in a pan. In a bowl, whisk together egg yolks, sugar and maple syrup. Mix in flour, then add to milk in the pan along with cinnamon stick. Warm over low heat, whisking non-stop, until the first bubble appears. Remove from heat and let cool completely. Remove cinnamon stick.

Divide mixture between doughed-lined muffin moulds. If desired, top with a few berries to taste. Bake for 10 minutes or until the crust is golden brown and the filling well caramelized.

Remove from oven and let cool. Sprinkle each tart with ground cinnamon and serve.

BASIC RECIPES
Receitas básicas

AIOLI

Aïoli

YIELD: 125 ML (1/2 CUP)
PREPARATION: 10 MINUTES

2 garlic cloves, chopped
2 egg yolks
1 tbsp piri-piri mustard (see recipe p. 205)
5 tbsp extra-virgin olive oil
Sea salt
Fresh ground black pepper

In a mortar, crush garlic using the pestle.

Transfer crushed garlic to a bowl, add egg yolks and mustard, then whisk vigorously with a fork to a creamy consistency. Add oil in a stream, whisking non-stop.

Once sauce is well thickened, season with salt and pepper.

LEMON & SAFFRON AIOLI

Aïoli de limão e açafrão

YIELD: 125 ML (1/2 CUP)
PREPARATION: 10 MINUTES

2 garlic cloves, chopped
2 egg yolks
1 tbsp piri-piri mustard (see recipe p. 205)
5 tbsp extra-virgin olive oil
Juice of 1/2 lemon
1 pinch of saffron
Sea salt
Fresh ground black pepper

In a mortar, crush garlic using the pestle.

Transfer crushed garlic to a bowl, then vigorously whisk in egg yolks and mustard to thicken into an aioli. Slowly drizzle in olive oil, whisking non-stop.

Once sauce is well thickened, season with salt and pepper, then pour in lemon juice and mix. Flavour sauce with a pinch of saffron.

APPLE WHITE BUTTER SAUCE

Manteiga de maçã

YIELD: 500 ML (2 CUPS)
PREPARATION: 5 MINUTES
COOKING: 10 MINUTES

1 tsp unsalted butter
2 shallots, minced
1 apple, peeled, seeded and grated, Cortland type
125 ml (1/2 cup) white wine
125 ml (1/2 cup) heavy (35%) whipping cream
115 g (1/2 cup) cold unsalted butter, small diced
Sea salt
Fresh ground black pepper

NOTE
Butter sauces are the perfect choice to dress up grilled fish.

In a skillet, melt butter, then cook shallots and apple over low heat. Add in white wine and let reduce by half. Pour in cream and let reduce again by half.

Add butter and whisk vigorously into a thickened sauce. Strain sauce through a fine sieve. Season and keep warm.

CHOURIÇO CHIPS

Chouriço croquante

SERVINGS: 4
PREPARATION: 5 MINUTES
COOKING: 10 MINUTES

1 *chouriço* (chorizo), thinly sliced into rounds

Preheat oven to 180°C (350°F). Line a cooking sheet with wax paper.

Layer *chouriço* slices on prepared cooking sheet. Cover with a second sheet of wax paper. To hold paper in place, weigh down with a second cooking sheet.

Bake in oven for 10 minutes, or until chips are golden-crisp, taking care not to burn them.

TOMATO JAM

Doce de tomate

YIELD: AROUND 4 JARS OF 250 ML (1 CUP)
PREPARATION: 20 MINUTES
COOKING: 3 HOURS

1 kg (2 lbs) tomatoes (preferably Italian)
720 g (3 2/3 cups) sugar
Zest of 1 lemon
1 cinnamon stick

NOTE
This jam will keep up to one year in the refrigerator or at room temperature if using a sealed jar.

Make an X-shaped cross at the base of each tomato.

Prepare a bowl of ice-cold water. Blanch tomatoes in a large pot of boiling water around 1 minute or until their skin bursts. Transfer them immediately to the bowl of icy water and let cool a few seconds. Peel off the skin using a small knife.

Lightly press down on tomatoes placed in a sieve on top of a bowl and let drain as much juice as possible.

In a pot, combine tomatoes, sugar, lemon zest and cinnamon stick. Simmer uncovered over very low heat for 3 hours, until the mixture turns jam-like, skimming the foam that forms on the surface from time to time.

Pour jam in previously sterilized jars and seal.

HERB-FLAVOURED FRESH CHEESE

Queijo fresco

YIELD: 2 CHEESE BALLS,
APPROX. 200 G (7 OZ) EACH
EACH PREPARATION: 10 MINUTES
RESTING: 3 HOURS
IN REFRIGERATOR

NOTE
Rennet is a natural coagulant essential to cheese-making. You can find Coalho em pó rennet in 20 g jars in Portuguese food stores.

4 L (16 cups) pasteurized cow milk (3.25%) or goat milk
1 jar (20 g) rennet (see note)
3 tbsp dried oregano (or other dried herb, to taste)
Sea salt

In a stainless steel bowl, combine pasteurized milk, rennet and oregano. Warm in a double boiler until liquid reaches 30°C (86°F). Remove from heat and let stand in double boiler for 20 minutes.

Stir gently for a few minutes, until preparation starts to curdle and thicken. Drain in a fine sieve placed over a bowl.

To give cheese its final shape, mould using 2 metallic cookie cutters and place on a perforated sheet to drain excess water. Season with salt on both sides and place in refrigerator to rest for 3 hours.

This cheese can be eaten fresh or chilled in refrigerator for up to 3 to 4 days, wrapped in plastic wrap.

PIRI-PIRI OIL

Azeite de piri-piri

YIELD: AROUND 750 ML (3 CUPS)
PREPARATION: 5 MINUTES
CONSERVATION: AROUND
6 MONTHS IN A COOL, DRY PLACE

150 g (1 cup) hot chili peppers (preferably bird's eye peppers), each cut in 2
500 ml (2 cups) extra-virgin olive oil
3 sprigs thyme
1 tbsp sea salt

Combine all the ingredients in a bowl. Divide among pre-sterilized jars. Keep in a cool place.

PIRI-PIRI

Piri piri

Piri-piri is simply the Swahili word for "pepper pepper." These small, easy-to-find peppers are used almost ubiquitously in Portuguese cuisine. You'll find them used whole, or as pepper sauce, in most of these recipes. Either way, piri-piri enhances flavour by giving food a little heat, a tangy, vibrant taste, and a dash of the exotic. In Portugal, piri-piri is that small, go-to ingredient that turns any dish into a celebration.

PICKLED VEGETABLES

Legumes em conserva de vinagre

YIELD: 6 X 500 ML JARS (2 CUPS)
PREPARATION: 25 MINUTES
COOKING: 30 MINUTES

500 ml (2 cups) water
500 g (2 cups) pearl onions
1 L (4 cups) white vinegar
400 g (2 cups) sugar
2 tbsp coarse salt
1 tbsp celery seeds
1 tbsp mustard seeds
1 tsp peppercorns
3 bay leaves
500 g (4 cups) green beans, cut in 5-cm (2-in) lengths
210 g (2 cups) cauliflower, sliced
270 g (2 cups) carrots, cut in small rounds
250 g (2 cups) cucumber, cut in small rounds

NOTE
Since the vinegar acts here as a preservative, wait at least 24 hours before eating pickled vegetables.

In boiling water, sterilize 6 glass jars of 500 ml (2 cups) each. Preheat oven to 180°C (350°F). Prepare a bowl of icy water.

Pour 500 ml (2 cups) water into a pot and bring to a boil. Blanch pearl onions for 30 seconds. Remove with a slotted spoon and transfer to the bowl of icy water. Drain and peel. Set aside.

In a pot, combine vinegar, sugar, coarse salt, celery seeds, mustard seeds, peppercorns and bay leaves. Bring to a boil for 5 minutes. Add vegetables, bring back to a boil and let simmer for 5 minutes. Remove pot from heat. Drain vegetables and set aside cooking liquid.

Divide vegetables between the 6 sterilized jars, packing them to within 2 cm (¾ in) of the top.

With a funnel, pour hot cooking liquid on the vegetables to within 1 cm (½ in) of the top. Using a rubber spatula, press down on the vegetables to remove air bubbles in the liquid. Wipe the mouth of the jar, if needed, then close lid without tightening too hard.

Put jars in a roasting pan and fill with water halfway up the jars. Sterilize in oven for 10 minutes. Remove from oven and let cool fully.

HOMEMADE MAYONNAISE

Maionese caseira

YIELD: AROUND 500 ML (2 CUPS)
PREPARATION: 15 MINUTES

3 egg yolks
1 tbsp Dijon mustard
1 tbsp lemon juice
1 tsp salt

125 ml (1/2 cup) extra-virgin olive oil
125 ml (1/2 cup) vegetable oil
1 tbsp parsley, chopped

NOTE
For a spicy mayonnaise, simply add 1 tbsp of piri-piri sauce to the ingredients before emulsifying. This mayonnaise will keep for up to 1 week in the refrigerator.

In a small bowl, whisk together egg yolks, mustard, lemon juice and salt until smooth.

To ensure a perfect emulsion, slowly pour in both oils in a small stream, alternating between them as you whisk non-stop. Once the mayonnaise starts to set, pour all remaining oil in a small drizzle, whisking continuously for 5 minutes or until the mayonnaise turns thick and very smooth. Add parsley.

PIRI-PIRI MUSTARD

Mostarda com piri-piri

YIELD: AROUND 250 ML (1 CUP)
SOAKING: 2 HOURS
PREPARATION: 10 MINUTES
CONSERVATION: 1 MONTH IN REFRIGERATOR

60 g (1/3 cup) mustard seeds
60 ml (1/4 cup) water
3 tbsp red wine vinegar
2 tbsp parsley, chopped
2 tbsp maple syrup (or honey)
3 tbsp all-purpose flour

1 tbsp piri-piri sauce
1 tsp brown sugar
Sea salt
Fresh ground black pepper
2 tbsp extra-virgin olive oil

In a bowl, soak mustard seeds in 60 ml (1/4 cup) water and 3 tbsp red wine vinegar around 2 hours. In blender, combine mustard seeds with their soaking liquid and remaining ingredients except olive oil. On lowest speed, blend while adding olive oil in a small, steady stream so that mustard will set rapidly.

Transfer this mustard to an airtight container and keep chilled in refrigerator.

CHICKPEA PURÉE

Pure de grão de bico

YIELD: AROUND 500 ML (2 CUPS)
PREPARATION: 10 MINUTES

1 can (540 ml/19 oz) plain chickpeas, rinsed and drained
    (see recipe below if using dry chickpeas)
4 tbsp tahini (sesame butter)
Juice of 2 lemons
2 garlic cloves, chopped
1 dash extra-virgin olive oil
1 small bunch fresh parsley, chopped
1 tsp mild paprika
Sea salt

In blender, mix chickpeas, tahini, lemon juice, garlic and a little salt until very smooth and creamy. If purée is too lumpy or thick, add a little of the chickpea liquid from can or a little water, one spoonful at a time, until desired consistency.

Transfer this purée to a serving dish, drizzle with a dash of olive oil, then sprinkle with chopped parsley and a pinch of paprika.

SOAKING AND COOKING DRY CHICKPEAS

PREPARATION: 5 MINUTES
SOAKING: 8 HOURS OR OVERNIGHT
COOKING: 1 HOUR

215 g (1 cup) dry chickpeas
2.5 L (10 cups) cold water
1 whole onion
2 bay leaves
Sea salt

Place chickpeas in a large salad bowl or pan (because they will swell considerably). Pour in water and let soak at room temperature at least 8 hours or overnight.

Drain chickpeas and rinse well. Transfer them to a large pot filled with at least 3 times their volume of water. Add onion, bay leaves and salt. Bring to a boil and cook at a rolling boil for 2 or 3 minutes, then reduce heat and cook uncovered around 1 hour 15 minutes, skimming regularly.

Use these cooked chickpeas to prepare the purée above. You can also add them to salads or stews.

TARTAR SAUCE

Molho tártaro

YIELD: 190 ML (3/4 CUP)
PREPARATION: 10 MINUTES
CONSERVATION: AROUND 1 WEEK
    IN REFRIGERATOR

125 ml (1/2 cup) homemade mayonnaise (see recipe p. 205)
2 tbsp parsley, chopped
2 tbsp red onion, chopped
2 tbsp cucumber, diced very small
1 tbsp capers, drained and chopped
1 tbsp Dijon mustard
1 tsp piri-piri sauce
Sea salt
Fresh ground black pepper

In a bowl, combine all the ingredients. Transfer this sauce to an airtight container and chill in refrigerator for up to 1 week.

Serve with cod cakes, fish and chips-style cod (see recipe p. 78), or pan-seared or grilled fish.

GOOD ADDRESSES
Helena Bons endereços

Le Cantinho de Lisboa
356 Saint-Paul St. West, Montreal, Quebec H2Y 2A6
514-843-3003

La Vieille Europe
3855 Saint-Laurent Blvd., Montreal, Quebec H2W 1X9
514-842-5773

Les Anges Gourmets
4247 Saint-Laurent Blvd., Montreal, Quebec H2W 1Z4
514-281-6947

Boucherie & Épicerie Soares & Fils
130 Duluth Av. East, Montreal, Quebec H2W 1H1
514-288-2451

ACE Quincaillerie Azores
4299 Saint-Laurent Blvd., Montreal, Quebec H2W 1Z4
514-845-3543

Épicerie Européenne
560 Saint-Jean St., Quebec City, Quebec G1R 1P6
418-529-4847

Gastronomie signée Marie-Chantal Lepage
1 Wolfe Montcalm St., Quebec City, Quebec G1R 5H3
418-644-6780

Gourmande de nature
1912 Chemin de l'Étang-du-Nord, Magdalen Islands,
Quebec G4T 3C7
418-986-6767

RECIPE INDEX

Indice de receitas

Hors d'oeuvre & Starters

Black-Cod Gravlax, 24

Braised Squid, 17

Leek & *Chouriço* Tarts, 28

Lobster Rolls With Fresh Vegetables, 23

Octopus Carpaccio With Citrus, 18

Peppers Stuffed With Goat Cheese, 31

Petiscos Platter, 13

Presunto & Cheese-Stuffed Bread Loaf, 27

Reinvented Seafood Terrine, 35

Sardine Balls, 14

Tuna, Sardine & Crab Rillettes, 32

Soups & Salads

Alentejana Gaspacho, 39

Asparagus Salad With Roasted Almonds, São Jorge Cheese & Serrano, 47

Caesar-Style Salad With *Chouriço* & Sardine Dressing, 61

Green Pea & Radish Salad, 52

Lobster, Cauliflower Semolina, Cilantro & Clementine Salad, 48

Octopus & Broad Bean Salad, 51

Pickled Sardine & Green Apple Salad, 56

Roasted Potato Salad, 55

Stone Soup, 43

Summer Vegetable Soup With Romano Beans, 40

Tomato Velouté, 44

Warm Endive Salad, 62

Fish

Cod & Sweet Potato Cakes, 67

Cod Omelette, 81

Cod With Green Peas & Poached Eggs, 71

Cod, Potato & Broccoli Casserole, 68

Cornbread-Crusted Cod, 77

European Sea-Bass Stew, 85

Fish and Chips-Style Cod, 78

Grilled Red Snapper With Parsley Sauce, 89

Monkfish & Clam Rice, 86

Sablefish Curry, 74

Swordfish Pica-Pau, 82

Seafood

Bulhão Pato Pasta, 108

Clams & *Chouriço*, 107

Creamy Lobster & Shrimp Rice, 115

Fish & Shrimp Pasta, 111

Grilled Seafood With Herb-Garlic Sauce, 101

Paella With Squid Ink Rice, 104

Seafood Stew, 112

Seafood-Stuffed Cabbage Rolls, 97

Shrimp With Port, 98

Shrimp, *Chouriço* & Roasted-Pineapple Kebabs, 94

Squid Bouillabaisse, 93

Meat & Poultry

All-Dressed Croque Monsieur, 123

Baked Pork Ribs, 120

Beef With *Chouriço* & Bean Stew, 119

Chicken À *Braz,* 142

Chicken Sausage Meatballs With Apples, 138

Cornish Hen & Clams, 145

Lamb Shanks With Red Wine, 130

Lamb Tartare, 137

Marinated Quails & Oven-Roasted Potatoes, 141

Marinated-Pork Sandwiches, 134

Pork Tenderloins With Port & Blueberry Sauce, 126

Rabbit Fricassee With Olives, 129

Rabbit in Mustard Sauce, 133

Sides

Confit Cherry Tomatoes, 168

Cornbread, 158

Cream of Green Pea Soup With *Chouriço* Chips, 153

Eggplant Caviar-Stuffed Tomatoes, 171

Oven-Baked Potatoes, 161

Oven-Baked Stuffed Potatoes, 162

Portuguese Blood Pudding With Rice, 149

São Jorge Cheese Shortbreads With *Chouriço* &
    Olives, 165

Spaghetti Squash With Tomato & Fresh Cheese, 150

Sweet-Potato *Migas,* 157

Two-Potato Gratin, 154

Desserts

Angel Food Cake, 184

Berlin Balls, 176

Fieldberry Crème Brûlée, 179

Heavenly Cream, 180

Maria Cookie Pie, 188

Meringue & Chocolate Mousse Domes, 183

Milk Tarts, 192

Orange-Thyme Pound Cake, 187

Pear-Almond Pie, 191

Portuguese Maple Pie, 195

Sugar Doughnuts, 175

Basic Recipes

Aioli, 198

Apple White Butter Sauce, 199

Chickpea Purée, 206

Chouriço Chips, 199

Herb-Flavoured Fresh Cheese, 201

Homemade Mayonnaise, 205

Lemon & Saffron Aioli, 198

Pickled Vegetables, 204

Piri-Piri Mustard, 205

Piri-Piri Oil, 201

Tartar Sauce, 207

Tomato Jam, 200

HEARTFELT THANKS
Agradecimento profundo

Making this book challenged me in every way, and proved a colossal task which I came to relish so very much!

From the bottom of my heart, I wish to thank my family first and foremost. Dinis, Daniel, Diogo, Stefanie and Nicky, I can be myself with you. Your love and support, your critical eye and knowledge sustain me on a daily basis. My greatest joy comes from sharing my table with you.

An extra special thank you goes to Nicky Cayer. You came as if on the wings of an angel and bolstered me up throughout this adventure of mine.

Jasmine McLean, my friend, thank you for your support and the magic of your words.

Many thanks also to my friend Jean-Paul Grappe, a great chef and fishing afficionado with an impressive track record, who kindly presented me to Mr. Pierre Bourdon.

My deepest appreciation goes to the great family that is Éditions de l'Homme. Thank you in particular to Pierre Bourdon, both a great businessman and visionary who put his trust in me; to Émilie Mongrain for your warmth, human side and precious counsel; to Josée Amyotte, who so perfectly understood who I am on that first day, then succeeded in translating my personality and vision to paper.

I also wish to thank the whole team at Tango, especially photographer Guy Arsenault. Your stunning pictures made my food look larger and more beautiful than life. Thank you also to food stylist Jacques Faucher for his undeniable talent; your professionalism, style and vision are unique (plus, I love your tableware collection!).

Many thanks to my associates Dinis Seara, David Barros, Jorge Jr and Jorge Da Silva, for your unfailing support and efforts day in, day out.

And finally, my gratitude goes out to the marvelous brigades at my restaurants—Helena, Portuscalle and Cantinho de Lisboa—who enter my kitchen and honour my table. My heart goes out to Manuel Da Silva, Travis Yee, Derek Bocking, Maxime Bedu, Valerie Van Audenrode and Maxime Méthé.

Chef Helena